THE RAPIST FILE

THE RAPIST FILE

Les Sussman and Sally Bordwell

with an introduction by

Ellen Frankfort

CHELSEA HOUSE
New York, London
1981

Library of Congress Cataloging in Publication Data

Sussman, Les, 1944-
  The rapist file.

  1. Rapists--United States--Interviews.
I. Bordwell, Sally, 1947-   . II. Title.
HV6561.S93   364.1'532'0973   81-10269
ISBN 0-87754-094-2   AACR2

Chelsea House Publishers
Harold Steinberg, Chairman & Publisher
Andrew E. Norman, President
Susan Lusk, Vice President
A Division of Chelsea House Educational Communications, Inc.
133 Christopher Street, New York 10014

CONTENTS

ACKNOWLEDGMENTS

We want to thank the many people who aided us in completing this book, who offered encouragement, provided information and expertise, and, when necessary, assumed the role of gentle taskmaster: Jay Robert Nash and James Agnew, for their professional and personal support; Jim Davies, taskmaster emeritus; Adele Leone, agent and friend; Alan Grossman, for his sense of humor when it was most needed; Max and Frieda Sussman; Fred and Linda Bordwell; Cleo Bordwell; Dr. William Hicks, for psychiatric perspective; Margaritte Burgett; Joy Johannessen, our editor; Dave Harris, former warden of Green Haven Correctional Facility; Jerry Persilly and Sergeant Charles Nobile, Green Haven Correctional Facility; the Illinois Department of Corrections; Louisiana State Penitentiary personnel; The Lerner Newspapers, Chicago, Illinois; and Dave Mozee, former director of information, Chicago Police Department.

INTRODUCTION

Ellen Frankfort

The men who speak with astonishing candor in this book are people who have taken woman-hating to its furthest possible point—the actual acting out on the body of that which other men do only in fantasy. An extreme statement? Yes, but rape is an extreme and violent act, and one of the most revealing aspects of this book is that a majority of the rapists interviewed here consider their actions neither violent nor extreme. Many do not even view themselves as rapists. One with a taste for nice distinctions insists that he is a sodomizer, not a rapist; others think of themselves as "lovers of women."

These are men who have kidnapped women, tied them up in bondage, shoved fists up their vaginas, penetrated them vaginally and anally with penis—and yet, as one puts it, "I didn't lay my hand on them and slap them around. I didn't slice them or nothin' like that—slice her up with a knife or shoot her or somethin' like that." Another man says, "No, I didn't see myself as a rapist, even when I saw a woman struggling, spread-eagled and tied down. . . . My idea of a rapist is a tree jumper—a guy that snatches a woman off the streets in dark alleys and in the parks." And then there's the one who thinks that a rapist is "someone who's done something terribly immoral, like raping a mother or killing a family."

Think about it: to rape, sodomize, ram fists and Coke bottles up the vagina of a woman is not violent, immoral or even extreme—unless the woman is a mother with a big family hanging by her apron strings. It almost makes rape sound wholesome.

Moreover, many of these rapists assume that similar attitudes are shared not only by their peers—". . . most [inmates] consider that psychotic, extreme form of rape is

3

rape. If I was to tell them about my case, they wouldn't view it as rape"—but by society at large, at least as embodied in the law. As one says, "And being that narcotics is a more powerful charge than rape . . . they pushed the rape charge on the side and got me with the drug charge." Another is convinced that the rape alone wouldn't have put him in prison: "She grabbed my hand where the meat fork was. . . . It happened to puncture her neck, and that's what got me convicted."

Are all rapists this nonchalant about their crimes? No. After listening to several talk (reading these interviews feels like listening to a conversation), I am convinced that there are differences among rapists. I'm even tempted to divide them into two basic categories: those who rape strictly for the pleasure of harming and humiliating a woman, and those who, isolated from people, especially women, see rape as a desperate means of having sex (these are often Southern white rural and religious men, to judge from the present sample). But there's a problem with dividing rapists into the violent type and the shy type, or Type A and Type B. For although the reflections of the two groups vary enormously, their actions do not. See if you can tell the difference between the violent and the shy rapist based on what each says.

"I would hit them, strip them, rip their clothes off, and stick them in front of a mirror. I'd hold their mouth and stick a knife in their chest while they were awake. . . . Yeah, that made me very hot—watching their reactions being stabbed or the breast cutting open." Type A, right? Right. This man numbers his victims "in the hundreds" and admits to having murdered twenty-five of them.

Then there's the rapist who says, "I didn't want to hurt the women—I wanted the women to love me is what it was." Type B, clearly. This sensitive fellow, according to the authors, has the look of a Rhodes scholar, right down to his Ben Franklin glasses, and is in fact a college graduate. But let's examine what this shy rapist did in order to gain the love he sought. There was no violence, he says, which is fine if you skip over the preceding sentences about sticking Coke bottles up the woman "and that kind of stuff." "That kind of stuff" for our scholarly lad turns out to be tying girls to beds, shaving their pubic hair, and raping them.

4

And lest you still believe that men with gentle politics will be gentle towards women, listen to another convicted rapist. "I said, 'You can't kill this woman. You didn't go to the Vietnam War because you didn't want to kill.'" But for some reason, women in bed are exempt from his nonviolent philosophy. He can do violence to them without (or despite) pacifist sympathies, and he does. Repeatedly.

It seems to amount to this: rapists vary in their degree of articulateness, understanding, and remorse—differences that shine through their own accounts. But what shine through with an even more compelling clarity are the assumptions made by *both* types about why men rape.

"It wasn't because I couldn't get sex. . . . In a way it was a thrill for some reason because they were scared. You know—'I gotcha.' They didn't want to do it, and that's what really turned me on. I was makin' them do something they didn't want to do. . . . If they cried it was just a bigger kick. . . . That's what the goals of rapists are—to humiliate." Another man puts it more succinctly. "I figure if you're not going to give it to me, then it's my right to take it."

The phrase "my right" stands out because it is repeated in one form or another by so many of the men who were interviewed. The assumption is that a woman's body is a man's *right,* and if violence occurs while the rapist is exercising that right (the act itself not being defined as violence, remember), it is because the woman attempts to deny him his due. In the case of rape, right justifies might. "It's always in a situation where the question is whether or not we're going to have sex," says one rapist, an educated man from a well-to-do family. "And if they say no, it's usually I say yes, and it ends up the act is committed." The language here is significant: a woman's resistance violates the natural order of things, "and it ends up the act is committed." What else?

The beauty of letting people speak for themselves is that there is no need to theorize, speculate, hypothesize. For years, feminists have been saying that putting a woman on a pedestal is the flip side of the coin that denigrates her. Perhaps it's more convincing coming from a convicted rapist. "I had a definite image of a female in my mind. A kind of goddess-on-a-pedestal sort of thing. See, it goes back even farther than I can remember, to when I was a kid in grammar school adoring the blessed Virgin Mary thing they used to beat into you. In a way this was also in my mind—to fuck the blessed Virgin Mary."

Even when the speaker is trying to be sincere in analyzing motivation, his ability to delude himself amazes. One man lectures with authority on "the law of the rapist." "If they conduct theirself as a lady, clean-cut and what have you, they don't have to worry about any of this. If they conduct theirself as a hussy, then they got it coming by the law of the rapist." And what is this law? Quite simply: "Get anybody that's asking for it." Hence you might conclude that this man raped some seductively posed, scantily clad "hussy" he found perched on a stool in a sleazy bar. Not so. This man raped the sixty-three-year-old wife of his boss in her home—where, he complains, she went quite a bit beyond the call of duty in terms of lady-like behavior by "just lay[ing] there like a dead person." So much for the Law of the Rapist.

Again, it's the language that provides the reliable clues. "I used to go into women's stores," begins one rapist, "and when I see something that's appealing to me . . ." Some*thing*. A dress? A pair of shoes? Or was it a pair of tits, a cunt? For the rapist, all these things are detached from the human, from the living, from the whole person; naturally, the some*thing* was a woman. Men talk repeatedly in this book of getting "it" from women as if "it" were a slit painted on a mannequin. One all-American college type speaks of the most beautiful "thing" on campus. He is not referring to a new running track.

The objectification of women into parts detached from any whole human being is at the heart of pornography. Yet most rapists are moralists; they strongly oppose pornography. "You should concentrate on what brings about rape," says one. "Rape is a sexual and violent act. If you were sexually oriented in this society and then turned to something violent—this is where you get your rapist from. . . . That's why I don't go to a lot of them movies . . . nothing but X-rated films—nothing but sex, people in bed. I don't call that sex. That's a complete distortion. . . . The next scene is more murder. That's an orientation . . . then, you got yourself a rapist." There's an irony here that's hard to miss: if convicted rapists were to mount a campaign against pornography, would

6

they be dismissed on civil libertarian or any other grounds as readily as are feminists?

I doubt that the publishers of men's magazines view their products as manuals for rapists. And yet, according to one rapist, he did not learn about bondage from his buddies on the street but "out of *Penthouse* magazine. I never knew about that until I read that magazine." Another, assuming the air of a detached professional, states, "I ran a photography and filmmaking studio. [When I get out] I'm going into pornography. I'll probably deal with sadomasochism and rape. . . . They [his victims] wasn't into bondage, they wasn't into anal sex, and I just introduced it to them. That's how I see it."

Whether they condemn it or use it to rationalize their actions, most rapists recognize pornography as a way of lending legitimacy to what they know better than anyone is not legitimate. "Everywhere you go there's pornography. The mentality of the young is being infested." Now, this is not a Bible Belt preacher or a feminist speaking; it's a convicted rapist, one of several in this book who started their careers as pimps. "The old man says if you want to be a good pimp, you always got to sodomize them . . . hurt her, afflict her. . . . So I did it."

But you don't have to be a pimp to perceive a relation between pornography and rape. Feminists state it this way: pornography is the theory, rape the practice. Here's a college graduate, who also happens to be a convicted rapist, on the subject: "I've dreamed so many times of speaking to thousands of women. I'd talk about the porno industry that seems to have brought a lot of moral change about. . . . There might be less rapes going on because of the easiness of having sex with a woman. But at the same time, the guys who have been the nice dudes all their life, that all this exposure might bring them out of the closet. That's the fear I have. Where if they can't have that kind of easy relationship with a woman, this is going to make a rapist out of them."

What's interesting about these rapists—whether street-smart dudes or college grads—is their indifference to what are considered the conventional turn-ons in this society. Some claim to have refined preferences as to various parts of the body or to be interested only in "beauties," but by and large they're not out looking for a prom queen. "It wasn't so much the legs or anything else that excited me. . . . young, old, even babies sometimes crossed my mind."

7

Or "There ain't no special color. If they show me something, they can be green. I'm gonna get it." And it's not just color that he's indifferent to; this man says he started his career as a rapist at age nine, raped a seventy-eight-year-old woman at age fifteen, and has continued raping ever since, right through his time in prison. Assuming a somewhat jaunty air, he says, not without a touch of pride, "I ain't serving life like some inmates who are serving life for nothing. . . . Besides killin' or beatin' up, that's the next best thing I know—to rape."

If age, color, beauty are not the turn-ons, you might assume that at least the rape victim has to be female. Wrong. The rape victim has to have, as one rapist put it, femaleness. "They [other inmates] might go put on some tight pants, tie their head up. They're showing me that they got more female than anything. If I ask 'em for it and they don't give it to me, then there's only one thing left to do—and that's take it." So we're back to the old familiar refrain: if a man sees some*thing* he wants and can't have *it,* all he has to do is take *it.* In other words, a man has a right to bully another *thing* into submission as long as that other *thing* has "femaleness." And this is so whether he's on the streets or behind bars.

If this complex of attitudes partially explains why most rapists do not believe they've done anything extreme or "terribly immoral," it perhaps also throws light on their status within the prison hierarchy. On the one hand, the act in itself doesn't involve beating up or slicing up, and anyway, it's done against women, so what's the big deal? But by the same token that it's not really serious, it's also not a crime to which much prestige attaches in the male scheme of things. "The guys that commit murder, shoot little kids, and that stuff—they're in the top echelon. And then you have your bank robbers, forgers, that type of thing. And then the rapists," says one man bitterly. The rapist who winds up in prison is a man who was only exercising his rights but was dumb enough to get caught at it and sent up on account of a woman. Even the guy who's proud to be doing time for rape admits it's "the next best thing" to beating and killing.

There's another dimension to the rapist's position at the bottom of the prison pecking order. Macho crimes like murder undeniably exert a certain fascination, and almost everyone has some romantic regard for the outlaw who steals, especially if he redistributes the bounty fairly. But the rapist knows that what drives him on is nothing romantic—just pure hatred accompanied by the need to humiliate. "I couldn't stand her. I used to humiliate her. . . . I used to hit her in the ass with paper clips because I hated her, man," says one rapist of the teacher he attacked. And yet as soon as the object of hate stopped resisting, the pleasure faded. As the same man put it when asked why he turned off to a woman who said he could rape her, "I guess when someone has hostility built up in them, it makes it pressing, right? And if you play a game with yourself and then the game's exposed to you, you back away from it."

"Game exposed"? What does that mean? That the other person is on to you? That you are no longer the one calling the shots? That you do not dominate the victim? That the woman is no longer the victim? In contrast to many judges, doctors, and law enforcement officials, few rapists believe that women want to be raped. They know the truth because, as they state, they would not enjoy rape if the women did. For a long time feminists have been arguing that rape is an expression of hostility and that sexual attraction is often irrelevant. Yet I can still remember the young, liberal lawyer who questioned whether a man arrested for shoving his fist up a woman's vagina really did it, pointing out that the woman was not attractive and the man was. He could get plenty of women, so why would he choose her? the lawyer argued. Evidently he hadn't spent much time listening to rapists on the subject.

Many rapists in prison, including some who tell their stories in this book, will be back on the street again. As one who is now out on parole said, "I might do it again. There's no telling." This might-do-it-again theme recurs throughout the interviews. Indeed, many of the rapists are repeat offenders. "When you come here you do time, and that's it. They warehouse people. And when you leave it's gonna happen again" is a fairly typical response. On the whole, not a reassuring picture.

Then what are the practical tips we can learn from listening to the rapists themselves? Says one, "The best thing women can do is feel along, you know? . . . They might be able to sane the guy. They might be able to bluff him, like sayin', 'My husband lives right here' when she might live ten miles from here. Unless she is really sure she can overpower him physically, it would be best to submit. Because a guy is out to rape, not to do physical harm. The majority of guys I talked to, they wouldn't. I know I wouldn't. If you panic him, it's just like the burglar. If you scare the burglar he might turn around and shoot you. . . . I wouldn't advise a woman to scream. With me it worked. . . . But it's the same thing. You scream, you might scare him, and you could get hurt. If he's not up on you, scream and run. But if he's up on you, don't fight it. Submit." Makes pretty good common sense, I'd say. And here are a few more common-sense tips based on my overall impressions after reading these interviews—a composite, if you will.

Most rapists learn early on to carry a weapon, usually a knife or a gun. Frequently, it is because they know that the only way to insure a woman's submission is to threaten her with a weapon. They do not necessarily plan to use it, although some do. One man who insists he had no prior plans to kill came close to doing so when the woman said he could rape her but begged him not to kill her. It seems his sense of honor was offended.

I think the above-quoted speaker is on solid ground in advising women to follow their instincts. If you sense a shyness or hesitation, scream or tell the guy to fuck off. (One rapist said that the woman should have shamed him—a "What would your mother think?" sort of approach with a scolding finger.) Many men who rape believe that their victims are timid women (femaleness). Gutsy talk impresses them; they feel "exposed."

In small towns, cars are the only means of getting around; cars become convenient bedrooms when driven to a lonely spot. It is creepy to learn how many hours rapists spend cruising around casing out areas for rape victims. So: don't talk to anyone who slows down and follows you in a car. In the city, don't enter conversations on subways. Rapists, even the shyest, develop strategies. Getting a woman's attention, getting her to respond, is the biggest obstacle, reports one rapist, who overcame it by using a Polaroid camera. He knew the line "Haven't I seen you before?" was stale, so he would stand in the corner of a subway car, take a picture of a potential victim, and drop it in front of her. As he proudly notes, she couldn't help but respond. Even though she knew the picture didn't belong to her, she had to wonder how her face wound up on the subway floor.

Another of those my-mother-always-told-me tips: if I were living alone, particularly in a suburban community, I would think twice about taking a ground-floor apartment. Many rapists plan

10

carefully before they act, hiding while they check out when you get home, when you get undressed, how much of the window you leave open. A ground-floor apartment offers both ease of observation and ease of access.

If there is any one item that is most frequently mentioned as the provocation for rape, it is clothing. Of course we should be able to dress as we please, but clothing is a symbol, as the fashion industry itself understands all too well. And today more than ever, the inspiration for fashion seems to come from pornography: spiked heels, tight-assed jeans, shiny black satin blouses. Rapists are tuned in to the culture; like the rest of us, they pick up the signals from the tube, from the back of the bus. And although it is an infringement on our freedom not to be able to dress as we choose, it is also true that by avoiding certain types of clothing, we can boycott the influence of chic misogyny—in a fashion at the very least, and hopefully in a few rapists.

These are times when the combat look serves a real warrior function (although it is more a reflection of the boutiquing of America than any concern for women's freedom that has us wearing fake jungle camouflage tops and hiking boots). Most rapists seem to be seeking docility; army fatigues, baggy pants, and running shoes do not suggest docility. Think of the difference it would make if you were wearing spiked heels rather than running shoes when you wanted to walk away, quickly but without signs of panic, from some guy cruising by you in a car.

Indeed, the no-frills look associated with strong, independent women may be the best deterrent of all. To feel at ease with one's body is probably better than all the mace. It seems that what rapists respond to isn't something physical so much as something psychological—call it karma, vibes, whatever. Clothing that says, "I am not dressing for you, man, but for myself" does not speak a message of meekness.

Feminists have always said that rape transcends class lines. If, however, you still think of a rapist as someone with bloodshot eyes whom you might run into on the A train in New York, listen to what one rapist said when asked if women are being misinformed about rapists. "Sure. They're seeing them jumping out of trees, behind bushes, comin' up out of the back of cars. In the last five or ten years this, it

11

seems, is what has really been brought to the public's eyes. But it's the everyday guy you wouldn't really suspect—the bank teller, the nice guy, the eight-to-five guy who holds a job. Those people have more tendency to be latent rapists than anybody to my knowledge, and it's been discussed in length with different people—fraternity brothers, college professors, whatever, guys that I have known personally that could be potential rapists."

What is the moral, then? After reading *The Rapist File,* I would say the moral is that any man can become a rapist, including your college professor—or your husband or lover, for that matter, as recent trials have shown. What makes this book so valuable is that you get a feeling for just how individual each rapist is. Each has his reasons, his relations to his mother, his early sex life; in other words, each carries around his own particular psychic baggage. Some are more articulate, as I said, and some are even more likable than others. Having thus been made human, the rapist is no longer an abstraction; he is real. And so, while I wound up liking some and hating others—feeling that with this one, I could talk my way out of it, with that one, forget it, I'd be lucky to get out alive, and knowing with at least one that there was nothing I could have done to spare my life—*all,* I had to remember, were convicted rapists.

Being able to listen to them speak is an eerie privilege; I learned a lot. But there is no way to finish this book without being horrified. In the final analysis, it does not matter whether we wear combat boots or running shoes and destroy every pair of tight jeans and spiked heels. For who among us might not be that woman who, as her rapist put it, "just happened to be in the wrong place at the right time"? As the rapists themselves make clear through their actions and words, the desire to harm women is so profound in our culture that the only sure way to prevent rape is by a revolution of consciousness. Without an entire transformation of the power relationships between men and women as we currently know them, men are going to continue to inflict physical harm and to rape, no matter what. If you have any doubts, just listen to what the rapists say.

And listen to them we must. In no other way are the

dark shadows that frighten us at night, the ghosts that make living more terrifying, going to disappear. The first step in overcoming fear is to gain knowledge, to demystify, to make real the abstract. This book does just that.

AUTHORS' INTRODUCTION

This book began in a modestly furnished apartment on Chicago's Northwest Side, a working-class neighborhood comprised of two-flats and single-family homes. The ex-rapist who sat chatting with us while his pregnant wife served coffee was the first of dozens of rapists we would interview in the months that followed—interviews that took us on a crisscross journey through the American landscape, to penitentiaries located in the country-club setting of upstate New York, amidst lonely acres of Midwestern cornfields, and in the eerie dankness of Southern bayous.

It was in such penitentiaries that we sat for hours upon end listening to brutal tales of rape and sexual deviation. There were moments, locked up in hot, stuffy prison interview rooms, when the stories we heard filled us with outrage, horror, or revulsion. There were also times when we felt deep pity for human beings whose lives were so out of control. But whatever we felt, we tried our best to keep our emotions to ourselves. After all, we were there to listen, not judge, and to present to the reader the one voice that has been missing from most literature about rape—that of the rapist himself.

Rape is clearly a widespread social problem and is more common in the United States than in any other country in the modern world. According to FBI Uniform Crime Report statistics, there were an estimated 63,020 rapes or attempted rapes in the United States in 1977—which means that approximately one rape or attempted rape was committed every nine minutes. These figures are all the more disturbing in that they omit statutory rape and other types of sex offenses and represent only reported rapes. It is further estimated that fifty to ninety percent of all rapes or attempted rapes go unreported. Government statistics indicate that suspects are apprehended in only five percent of reported rape cases and that convictions are obtained in less than three percent of these.

15

The typical rape victim is under twenty-one. The typical rapist is also young, generally under thirty; most rapists arrested in 1977 were in the eighteen-to-twenty-two age bracket. Most often they attacked complete strangers or casual acquaintances, usually in the victim's home or on the street. To judge from reported cases, rapes occur most frequently in the summer months, rising to a peak in August.

As journalists, we wanted to know more about the individuals responsible for these statistics. We wanted to explore just what makes a rapist tick, to break down the stereotype of the rapist as malevolent superman and present him instead as a human being. In our effort to fathom the workings of a rapist's mind, we also hoped to offer some fresh insights into the phenomenon of rape.

The project was, from its inception, a challenging one. We were aware that except for a handful of psychiatrists and other clinical professionals, no one had ever tackled the task of interviewing rapists in state penitentiaries on the scale that we planned. In fact, surprisingly little has been written about the rapist himself—how he describes his motivations and accounts for his actions. As Susan Brownmiller noted in her classic study of rape, Eldridge Cleaver's *Soul on Ice* is one of the few books to offer a glimpse of this relatively unexplored terrain.

We wondered why this was so, and some of the reasons quickly became apparent—red tape and a morass of confusing prison regulations that made it difficult if not impossible to gain access to sex offenders. We found that prison officials were zealous in their efforts to protect inmates' rights, often to the point of paranoia. They politely refused repeated requests for the names of incarcerated rapists, and even when we knew the name of a particular rapist we wanted to interview, we were not permitted to contact him because we did not have his prison number. When we asked for the number, we were told that it was confidential and could not be released. It quickly became a Catch-22 situation at its most absurd. For several months we went around and around like this, even enlisting the help of a friendly state senator to no avail.

Such obstacles seemed almost insurmountable, and there were moments when both of us gave serious thought to abandoning the entire project. But there is a key to unlock every door, even every prison door, and eventually we hit upon two ideas that yielded results.

The first idea struck us upon reading a Chicago "underground" newspaper. To our astonishment, the back section of the paper contained a list of names and numbers of inmates seeking correspondence with anyone on the outside. It was a simple next step to write these inmates offering payment for each name and number of a rapist they supplied. Within two weeks, the long-sought information began to trickle in. We applied the same technique in other states where we decided to conduct interviews, contacting the local underground newspaper and taking it from there.

At the same time, we wrote the wardens of several penitentiaries to inquire if we could have a notice placed on prison bulletin boards advertising payment for information about the lives and crimes of sex offenders. The wardens responded affirmatively, stating that there were no regulations to prohibit the posting of such a notice. Another key turned, and another prison gate opened to us.

It did not take long for the first cautious queries from rapists to turn up in our mail. The two main concerns were confidentiality and the amount of money we planned to pay. We answered such letters with a standard reply: it was not necessary for the rapist to write anything; we would pay just for the opportunity of conducting personal interviews. Letters of agreement arrived quickly.

Within a matter of weeks we had a long list of rapists willing to participate in the project, and a short synopsis of their crimes. Several wrote claiming that they were innocent, and those letters we did not respond to. We wanted to talk to confessed hard-core rapists only, and to select as representative a batch as possible. From almost one hundred names, we chose the twenty-five rapists who seemed to have the most interesting case histories.

Once we had the necessary names and numbers, prison officials were more than cordial to us and even arranged special visiting privileges. Their only concern was whether we planned to do some kind of exposé of prison conditions, and we hastened to reassure them on this point. All the interviews were conducted jointly, except for those in Menard Correctional Center, where

17

officials refused to allow Sally into the psychiatric compound for fear that harm would come to her.

The time allotted for the interviews varied from prison to prison. In some cases we were given an hour per interview, in others only thirty minutes; the average interview lasted about forty-five minutes.

Although we did not follow a rigid format for each interview, there were certain questions we consistently asked—for example, what the rapists' relationships with their mothers were like, how they felt during and after each assault, and whether they believed that women want to be raped. Some rapists were talkative and seemed almost reluctant to have the interview end. It was as if they had never had an opportunity during their incarceration to speak so freely about a subject that was obviously preying on their minds. Others, however interesting their cases, were nervous or uncommunicative, and we found ourselves with abbreviated interviews. In the end, we went over our transcripts and chose the fifteen best interviews for purposes of this book. Because our subjects were guaranteed confidentiality, their names have been changed.

In the course of our research, we traveled to three states—New York, Louisiana, and Illinois—and interviewed rapists in three different prison systems. Each of these states has a different legal definition of rape, and we became aware of wide discrepancies in the laws governing the disposition of rape cases. Readers will note these variations in the brief description of crime and sentence that precedes each interview.

Generally speaking, the sentencing of a rapist is unpredictable at best. The judge not only has too little time but also too little information to deal effectively with each individual offender. Ordinarily he has at his disposal a psychiatric report (sometimes based on only one interview), a report from a probation officer, and a police record that is often incomplete. The capriciousness of sentencing is sometimes further encouraged by state law. Louisiana is an excellent case in point.

Louisiana's revised statute defines rape as "the act of anal or vaginal sexual intercourse with a male or female person who is not the spouse of the offender, committed without the person's lawful consent." Under this general rubric, the offender may be convicted of simple rape, forcible rape, or aggravated rape, depending on the circumstances involved in the case. Aggravated rape was a capital crime in Louisiana until 1974, when the U.S. Supreme Court declared Louisiana's mandatory death penalty for rape unconstitutional.* Aggravated rape in that state is now punishable by life imprisonment at hard labor without benefit of parole, probation, or suspension of sentence.

According to Louisiana's statute, a man can be convicted of aggravated rape in cases where "the victim is prevented from resisting the act by threats of great and immediate bodily harm, accompanied by apparent power of execution." Forcible rape, a less serious charge, is punishable by not less than two or more than forty years at hard labor. It applies in cases where "the victim is prevented from resisting the act by force or threats of physical violence under circumstances where the victim reasonably believes that such resistance would not prevent the rape." Clearly, Louisiana's distinction between aggravated rape and forcible rape is nebulous and open to argument. Thus, the current statute leaves plenty of room for inconsistent or indiscriminate sentencing, sometimes based on racial prejudice.

Rape in New York State and Illinois is punished far more leniently than in Louisiana and most Southern states. Under New York statutes, for example, a man is guilty of first-degree rape "when he engages in sexual intercourse with a female by forcible compulsion," which is defined as "physical force which is capable of overcoming earnest resistance; or a threat, expressed or implied, that places a person in fear of immediate death or serious injury to himself." Thus, a conviction for first-degree rape in New York is comparable to a conviction for aggravated rape in Louisiana. But while aggravated rape in Louisiana carries a mandatory life sentence, a first-degree rape charge in New York carries an indeterminate sentence of at least six years but not more than twenty-five years.

Currently the Illinois statute regarding rape does not recognize various kinds and degrees of sexual assault and is not broken

*Since 1930, 455 rapists have been executed in the United States; eighty-nine percent were black. After 1974, Georgia was the only remaining state where a conviction for the rape of an adult woman could result in the death penalty. In 1977, in *Coker* v. *Georgia,* the Supreme Court ruled that "the sentence of death is grossly disproportionate and excessive punishment for the crime of rape of an adult woman, and is therefore barred by the eighth amendment as cruel and unusual punishment." Currently, under Mississippi and Florida law, the death penalty can still be applied in cases involving the rape of a minor (twelve years old or under).

19

down into different categories, as are those of New York and Louisiana. The six-year minimum penalty for all degrees of rape in Illinois is the same as New York's minimum sentence for a violent first-degree rape conviction. Ostensibly this seems unfair only to the offender, but it is often even more unfair to the victim because it is far more difficult to obtain convictions under the Illinois statute. According to a report of the Illinois legislature's Rape Study Committee, "many judges are reluctant to hand down this sentence for certain rape offenses which they believe do not warrant such severe punishment."

Apart from the legal issues, what did we learn from our interviews with rapists? As we have said, we approached this project as journalists, with no intention of drawing scientific conclusions or making sweeping generalizations as to the nature of the rapist. Still, we did come away from the experience with some general impressions, which on the whole tally with available statistics.

A study conducted by the Law Enforcement Assistance Association (LEAA) in 1978 showed that in seventy percent of reported rapes, the assailant either threatened or actually employed force. With few exceptions, the rapists we interviewed admitted to using force, and most used a weapon of some sort, usually a gun or a knife. Some were less conventional, however—for instance, Harold, who toted a toy gun, or Dave, who occasionally brandished a broken bottle, or Ben, who threatened his victim with a meat fork. A few of our subjects who portrayed themselves as "lovers" rather than rapists conceded rather reluctantly that they forced their victims into submission; Julio, for example, describes the weapons he carried as "means of protection" and insists that they played no role in the rapes he committed.

In another LEAA study, headed by Dr. Edward Brescher, a substantial number of rapists reported being abused as children, not only physically, but sexually as well. Among the rapists we interviewed, Zeke is a particularly pathetic example of such sexual abuse. The son of a pimp, he was brutally sodomized as a child by one of his father's prostitutes; as an adult, he meted out exactly the same treatment to women. Another man, Ray, was not the target of sexual abuse himself, but he suffered the trauma of seeing his father repeatedly rape his mother with a Coke bottle; in his career as a rapist, Ray simulated his father's behavior.

Dr. Brescher's study also points to the lack or inadequacy of

20

treatment programs specifically geared to the rehabilitation of rapists. In our own research we came upon the unsettling truth that the vast majority of rapists today are receiving virtually no therapeutic care. They are warehoused in the same cellblocks as inmates serving time for nonsexual offenses, and they are paroled in the same manner. Even if a rapist is sent to a state hospital for treatment, in most cases the hospital fails to provide therapy tailored to his particular needs. Ben is a poignant example of the effect of merely warehousing sexual offenders. He has sought—and consistently failed to obtain—psychiatric help within the Louisiana prison system. As a result, he has taken the desperate measure of asking the state to permit him to be castrated.

Like many of our subjects, Ben is a rapist who suffers from a sense of social inadequacy and low self-esteem; he obviously wants and should get professional help. But what should be done with a man like Sal, who raped and murdered many times and would seemingly not hesitate to do so again? It is tempting to conclude that Sal is a hopeless case, but the fact remains that he is eligible for parole in 1999 and may well be back on the street without having received sustained psychiatric treatment. As Dr. Brescher points out, this situation is all the more illogical in that "the costs of providing relevant treatment are no higher than the costs of providing the irrelevant treatment currently provided."

If there is any single conclusion that can be drawn from our investigations, it is that rapists are as like and as different from one another as any other group of people. This is an obvious but important point that is all too often ignored in the search for easy explanations or pat formulas. Each rapist has his particular history and his particular set of perceptions of the world. Some of the rapists we interviewed blamed their crimes on "society," others on their parents or their victims; still others were at a loss to account for their actions. Some expressed deep remorse about what they had done, while others broadly hinted that they would rape again, given the opportunity. Some welcomed their victims' resistance as necessary to their own gratification, others were enraged by it, and others were frightened and backed off.

What you will hear in the following pages is not the voice of "the rapist," but fifteen highly individualized voices telling fifteen different stories. To our initial question "What makes a rapist tick?" they provide not one answer but many.

Part I

GREEN HAVEN
CORRECTIONAL FACILITY

It's a brisk, cloudy April morning, and we are driving along a winding two-lane road in upstate New York. Ahead of us looms Green Haven Correctional Facility, New York's largest maximum security prison, a formidable presence in the gently rolling countryside. There is a touch of the master illusionist about the layout of the place—the carefully manicured lawns, the neatly barbered hedges, the perfectly spaced trees lining both sides of the driveway. All in all, a neat bit of sleight of hand, the total effect obviously designed to convey a feeling of normality.

Leaving the car in the main parking lot, Sally and I make our way to the reception room, where friends and relatives of the inmates are conversing in hushed tones. The whole scene has a despairing atmosphere that even the panoramic view afforded by huge bay windows fails to dispel.

A brawny, bored-looking correctional officer inquires as to the nature of our business, and I tell him that we are here to conduct some interviews.

"Whatta yuh got there?" he asks, pointing to our equipment.

"Tape recorders," I say.

"You can't bring that in here."

"The warden okayed it," I protest, concealing my annoyance.

He eyes us suspiciously. "I gotta check with my superiors," he says, dutifully placing the call. "They got tape recorders with 'em," he tells whoever is on the other end of the line. There is a long pause. "Oh, I see. Thank you, sir." He carefully replaces the receiver.

"It's okay," he says almost begrudgingly. "But you gotta empty your pockets of anything in 'em that's metal."

We begin to unload, tossing keys, change, even credit cards on a counter. The guard watches disinterestedly.

"Awright, step through this," he says, indicating an airport-type metal detector. Sally passes through the electrified arch first, and an alarm buzzes like an angry hornet.

The guard shakes his head wearily. "What else yuh got on yuh that's metal?"

"Nothing," Sally replies nervously.

25

The guard tells her to remove her boots, which have metal zippers. "Awright, try it again." This time the alarm remains silent.

"It's the most sophisticated metal-detecting machine there is," the guard boasts as he motions me through. Hoping to be spared, I enter the arch. *Bzzzzzz.* In my case it proves to be the nails in the heels of my shoes that have triggered the sensitive device. I remove the offending footwear, and there is an approving silence from the metal sniffer.

Next the guard conducts a meticulous search of our equipment bags and spills the contents of Sally's purse on the counter, even making note of the number of tapes we have. Getting into Green Haven is almost as difficult as getting out, it seems.

Satisfied that we're not smuggling any contraband into the prison, he stamps our hands with some kind of invisible dye and pushes a hidden button. A steel door smoothly slides open, revealing yet another guard seated behind thick bullet-proof glass. We are asked to place our hands under an ultraviolet light. The stamp glows a psychedelic purple, and the guard opens a gate to a small courtyard that leads into the main penitentiary complex. There we are greeted by Sergeant Charles Nobile, a twenty-year veteran correctional officer, who is to be our escort. Nobile sometimes sounds more like a tour guide than a hard-boiled prison guard as he rattles off a storehouse of information about Green Haven. We learn from him the exact length of the prison corridors, the history of the penitentiary, and even the fact that the original Sing Sing electric chair is located on a top floor of the building we're now in.

As we enter the main prison complex, a huge gate ominously clangs shut behind us, seeming to separate us from everything safe and familiar. Nobile patiently waits for us to complete the final step of our processing—an identification check. We pass with flying colors.

"All set?" he asks with a grin as we walk away from the checkpoint, green visitors' tags clipped to our shirts.

"Yep, let's go see the warden."

Another gate yawns open, and we move even deeper into the heart of the penitentiary. Our nostrils are assailed by the strong scent of ammonia. We follow Nobile past a crew of inmates washing down a wall and go up a flight of stairs to the administrative offices. Everywhere, sullen eyes follow our progress.

Warden Dave Harris is not immediately on hand to welcome us. Instead, we are greeted by Jerald Persilly, Deputy Superintendent of Program Services. An amiable prison official who began his career as a parole officer in New Jersey, he says he hopes someday to be in charge of a joint like Green Haven. I can't help but silently wonder why.

We're about to have our second cup of strong prison coffee when Warden Harris walks into Persilly's office. He is a cheerful man with a baritone voice and a substantial frame. Sinking comfortably into a leather chair, he cordially inquires about our visit.

"Rapists," he says in answer to a question, "are not respected inside the prison. We got all the hard rocks here. Guys who hold up banks, shoot cops—macho types. They're respected, but not rapists."

We chat with the warden for a few minutes more, and then Sergeant Nobile enters to escort us to the old visitors' room, where we'll be interviewing the rapists. More gates clang, like an offbeat, off-key symphony orchestra. Gates within gates, some electronic, most operated manually. Whenever we pass a crew of inmates, they give us the once-over. Some stare unabashedly at Sally.

The old visitors' room is so named because some years ago a new and much more comfortable meeting area was constructed elsewhere in the prison. This relic is an oblong, pastel-colored room with an electronic gate at one end and a line of vending machines at the other. Two long rows of scarred wooden tables bisect the space, which is still very much in use.

Nobile shows us to a small cubicle where we set up our equipment, briefly review our notes, and wait for our first subject.

Zeke, age 24, was charged with attempted rape and conspiracy to sell narcotics. He received a five-to-ten-year sentence. He served a little more than five years at Green Haven Correctional Facility and was paroled on January 8, 1980.

"They was all asking for it. They'd flaunt themselves. And if I wasn't in the position to do it, somebody else would."

The visiting room has become crowded. Attorneys, their briefcases crammed with legal documents, are holding animated conversations with inmates dressed in prison greens. An elderly black woman tightly grips her son's hands across the wooden table. There are tears in her eyes. The two correctional officers on guard duty— one of them a young woman—appear to be relaxed.

The gate suddenly clangs open, and Zeke saunters into the small conference room. A young man of medium build, he wears his hair in an afro and has on a freshly pressed orange shirt. He shakes our hands with a confident grip and settles into a seat. When he smiles he displays a pearly row of teeth gapped at odd

29

intervals. A small scar courses down one side of his smooth-shaven cheeks.

Sally leads off with a question about Zeke's background. He tells her he was born in Los Angeles into what was considered a middle-class black family. He was the oldest of sixteen children, he says, and somewhere along the line he decided to move to New York City, where for eight years he operated a small photography studio.

"How was your relationship with your mother?" Sally asks.

"I didn't know my mother," he says grimly. "I still don't know her. I was raised by my father and various women."

"You mean women he was dating?"

He looks amused. "My father was a pimp, that's what I mean."

"How did that affect you as a child?"

"That's funny. To look back on it, I'd say it had quite a bit of an effect on me, because I'd seen all different types of women. All of them having me call them Mama was kinda strange to me when I started to realize this at nine years old—that I had so many different mothers and never really know my mother to today."

He smiles bitterly, perhaps at the irony of what he has just said. I note that Zeke chooses his words carefully and with deliberation. He also seems to avoid eye contact, instead scanning the room when he speaks.

"What did you really think of all these women?" Sally asks.

He ponders the question. "I thought it was kind of crazy. I had a kind of shocking blow at that time because they were all trying to say that my mother was this kind of woman and she was running around in the streets. I really couldn't believe it. I got turned off from women until I got about eighteen years old. I really despised women." He emphasizes the last few words.

"Wow, it was rough," he continues. "I couldn't actually blame one woman for what they did to me. That in itself is probably one of the reasons why I did a few things to them."

"Tell us about your first sexual experience."

"I was raped at the age of nine by a woman—I believe she was in her mid-twenties."

"Can you tell us more about it?"

Zeke nods but waits long seconds before answering, apparently reluctant to discuss this unpleasant incident. There's a harsh smile on his face as he begins.

"Well, we were playing around in a park one day, and I got all dirty and muddy. Her name was Shirley. She wanted to spank me because I got so dirty. So I told her at that time, 'You're not my mother. You have no right to spank me.'" Zeke makes rapid circular gestures with his hands as he speaks.

"So what she did, she sent me to my room, tied me down. She said, 'Now, you know I'm not your mother. You know what I do?' I said, 'I have a general idea of what you do. You take care of my father sexually and with money.' She says, 'Yes, I do, and now I'm gonna take care of you.'" Zeke shakes his head in disapproving remembrance before continuing.

"She got me all aroused and upset and did her thing. And that, I believe—I hate her to today for that. Because if it wasn't for my bein' tied down, I probably would have enjoyed it all. But she did what she wanted to do with me." His voice is punctuated with anger as he crushes out the butt of his cigarette and bums another one from Sally.

"What did she do to you?"

He wears an expression of distaste. "Well, she had me eat her—which I don't like—she used my body, she . . ." He pauses, hurt written on his face. "She . . . she put something in me—in my rectum." He falls silent and takes a deep pull on the cigarette.

"What did she put in you?"

Sally's question snaps him out of his reflective mood, and he shrugs, squirming uneasily in his chair. "I don't know. I can't go back to it. I'm trying to visualize it right now, the way it was. I can't figure out what it was, but it hurt. Then she got on me . . ." Zeke suddenly stops, as if the memory were getting the best of him.

"I tried to fight it at the time. I tried to tear the ropes that she tied me down with. But I couldn't get away. I . . ." He suddenly claps his hands to his bowed head. "I don't want to talk about it," he says.

Long moments pass. Sally finally interrupts the silence. "What was your relationship with her after that?"

Zeke seems to have recovered his composure. "After that incident she disappeared for awhile," he replies. "I seen her again when I was fourteen. She was in Saint Louis with another guy, but that guy was working for my father. I guess my father found out something about what she did and he sold her or whatever. I've seen her again off and on before going into the joint. I *despise* her."

"What was your next sexual experience?"

31

"I was eighteen. Yeah, that's when I enjoyed it. What I really enjoyed was when I tied them down. I tied this girl down in a position where she couldn't move. And I just used her. I did everything I wanted to do to her, as Shirley did to me."

"Did the girl struggle at all?"

He runs his fingers through his hair. "Yeah, she struggled because she didn't want to be tied down. I used my masculinity to overpower her—to tie her down secure—and I did what I had to do. I felt at that time it was my rightful payment for what had been done to me. This is why I took it out on her."

"Did the fact that she struggled turn you on?"

"Yeah." There is a note of defiance in his voice. "I said, 'This is what somebody did to me, let me see how you feel, how you like it, being that you're a woman and this is what you did to me.' I got gratification from it. I relaxed after I did it. As a matter of fact, I liked them all to struggle after that. Not literally to put bruises on them, but to tie them down and watch them struggle."

"What would you say to your victims?"

" 'It's too late now. I got you. You're mine to use the way I've been used, and there's nothing else to be said. You're not going anywhere. I have you.' " He spits the words out in staccato style, without a moment's hesitation.

Sally abruptly changes the subject. "Did you think the women would report you?"

He shrugs. "I had a few girls say that they was going to report me, but nothing happened. Because after two or three hours of having sex with them, even though it was forcible it was enjoyable."

"How many women did you actually rape?"

"Oh, six or seven between 1970 and 1972."

"Did you usually plan these or—"

"The last one that happened, I was at a disco. I seen this girl. It wasn't planned. I just wanted to make love to this girl. She turned me down, so I had to go into my burglary act. I followed her home, and I tried to force my way into her house about four o'clock in the morning. I took from her what I wanted. I tied her up."

"Did you beat her up?"

"Yeah, but if I put bruises on her I didn't see it."

"Did you use a weapon?"

Zeke shakes his head no.

"If these women you raped were in obvious pain, would that have turned you off?"

32

Again he shakes his head.

"Why not? Did you want to cause them pain as part of your revenge?"

A sullen expression seems to cloud his face. "Right," he says. "The pain part of it was the best part. Especially when I sodomized her. All six or seven of them. I had to get pain from entering them from behind. Because I had been entered in that way. It hurt me, and I knew it was going to hurt them."

Zeke becomes increasingly animated as he continues. "It was the pleasure of entering her from the ass. Because when I do that—even though I never had a virgin—if they never have been entered from the back, that's the virgin part of it. I just like to take that. That's a pleasure thing for me. I searched this whole world for a virgin and could never find one." He suddenly bursts into a fit of uncontrollable laughter. "The asshole, that's the only virgin part of a woman I could find," he says, guffawing again.

"So you liked to sodomize," I say.

He nods vigorously. "I think of myself as a sodomizer, not a rapist."

"What did the women you were sodomizing have to say about that?" Sally asks.

"They called me everything under the sun—black bastard, no-good nigger, faggot, homo—everything which someone would say if they was in pain," Zeke says, grinning.

I change the subject. "Did all these rapes take place in an apartment?"

"The last one took place in the park. The most women I grabbed, they was comin' out of the shopping center in the women's clothing department. That's where I centered most of my activities anyway. I never caught one just walking down the street or in the park. She'd always have to be in the store dressing herself—lingeries or stuff like that."

"Why's that?"

"I buy a lot of lingeries for women," he explains. "I got into the business of pimping four or five years ago. And I had to have a lot of women's clothing to bring out to the girls that operated for me." He pauses to ask Sally for another cigarette.

"I used to go into women's stores, and when I see something that's appealing to me and she doesn't want to submit to me, then I have this rage in me. I have to have her. She's the only one that's going to satisfy me. No matter where she's livin', I'll follow her there. I have to get her.

"Most of my activities took place at night. Because when I'd be like that I'd have to follow up women, sometimes up here to Westchester County—I'd have to follow her around all day until they go home. I'd go through my revenge. See, I'd have a cord in my car, and I would always put that in my pocket when I see a victim.

"Whenever I do come in contact with her, I try to make love with her—have her welcome me without forcing her. When she says no, or if she's married and brings up some tactics, then I have this rage that comes up in me again, and I might knock them down a few times. I'll get them around to somewhere—a chair or a bed— and I tied 'em down. And I would use them.

"I'd use the nylon cord. Also, I have wristbands that tennis players use. I would put them on so they wouldn't cut their arms struggling against the nylon band. Those bands would also protect me if I so happened to get picked up—if the girl called the police and said I did take her, raped her. It would show no scars on her if she says she was tied up. Nine out of ten times I made sure that they were unconscious when I left. I made sure of that."

"Did you ever rob your victims?"

He shakes his head. "I was never for the money. The money part was of no interest. Just the body."

"You thought you were such a good lover that the women you raped wouldn't report you, right?" I say.

"Yeah, I felt I was a good lover and that a woman wouldn't tell," Zeke casually replies. "But the first one, she didn't tell the police, she told her friends. I was wanted. The girlfriends' word of mouth went around, and there was a whole vigilante group all look- ing for me with guns. I got away from them to keep from getting knocked off. To keep the police from doing anything to me," he adds, "I made sure I wouldn't abuse my victims. I wouldn't put no scars on them. I'd slap 'em around and knock 'em out, but I'd never knock 'em out before I used their body."

"How could you tell whether your victims were alone?"

"I'd wait, and once I was inside the house I'd lock it up. I'd prop a chair under the doorknob in case the husband do come home, and make sure I'm next to a window. If somebody do unexpectedly come in on me, I'd go out the window." He flashes us a gap- toothed grin, as if proud of his ingenuity.

"Did that ever happen to you?"

"No one ever walked up to me, but once I heard a car comin' and I had to get away."

"Was there a particular type of victim you would single out?"

"All those with big asses," he says, smiling broadly at Sally.

"What about big breasts?" I ask.

This time he grins at me. "It didn't matter too much. I loved big asses, big thighs. The bottom turns me on."

I probe him further. "What about the way they dressed? What did you like your victims to wear?"

He chuckles. "Chic. I like clinging dresses, dungarees."

"Was there some kind of look or image you were after?"

Again he looks amused. "I was looking for a combination Sophia Loren and Jackie Kennedy," he says, breaking into a hearty laugh.

"The women you raped looked like the woman who raped you when you were a kid, didn't they?" I ask.

The question has its effect. Zeke falls into a somber mood as he mulls it over. "You know, they did," he finally replies, raising his eyebrows in amazement, as though the comparison had never occurred to him. "Because she had a big ass, the one that raped me. And all those I go for are built like that." He pauses to reflect on the matter for a few more seconds.

"What went on in your mind when you were trailing your victims?"

"I was thinking about how I was going to approach them, whether I should come on as most of the guys have been comin' on to her all day long—say, 'Hey, haven't I seen you someplace before?' But then I'd think to myself, I'm not goin' to come on to her like that. I'm goin' to wait until she come home, knock on the door, and once that door's open, there's no way she can close it on me."

"So you didn't speak to them, you just waited?"

"Most of them I waited until they got to their apartments. Two or three of them, I talked to them before. They promised me, 'I can't do it tonight, my boyfriend's here,' and things of that nature."

He pauses for a moment before continuing. "In the overall, I'd find out they was tellin' me a story, and once I followed them home they were home by themselves. That there would make me mad, plus the fact that she was the intended victim. All those who I have taken I do remember. I try to keep them separate in my mind and justify my act, because they all did turn me off from being

35

gentle," Zeke says earnestly.

"I would get enraged, angry, when they would start to tell me to get out of their house. They would get angry, and I'm trying to be nice—tell them that we have two or three hours together or things to this nature. And they would start screamin', and I would just go off—I'd knock them and slap them around, do my thing of tying them up." He falls silent on a not too gentle note.

Sally poses the next question. "Do you believe women in general ask to be raped?"

He ponders briefly. "I'd say about twenty percent of women want to be raped. Forty to sixty percent subconsciously want to be raped."

"Do you think the women you raped subconsciously wanted to be raped?" Sally pursues.

Zeke thoughtfully rubs his chin. "Yes."

Sally gives him a dubious look. He ignores her.

"How so?" I ask.

"I'd be seein' 'em walkin' the streets," he answers, gesturing with one hand as he speaks. "Various guys would be hittin' on them. Or the way the woman picks her clothes off the shelves and the way she looks at them. She'll be messin' with the lingerie or things of that nature. There's a certain way you can tell that a woman wants to have sex, you know?"

I shrug noncommittally. "Go on."

"When I approached—I approached one that was lookin' at nightgowns. She was lookin' at them all with them bedroom eyes. That look said she was lookin' for someone tonight. And as I approached her, as I asked her some off-the-wall question—'Haven't I seen you before?' or 'Aren't you so-and-so's sister or cousin?'— they would tell me no, and I'd be lookin' at them. And they'd be fiddlin' with them nightgowns or panties, and that's tellin' me right there that they want sex, but not particularly from me at that time. And that's when I let them go about their business, and I'd watch them all day long."

"Did you think of yourself as a rapist at that time?"

He shakes his head. "I was thinking of myself as a man who had to have a woman forcibly, and with her having to be tied down. No, I didn't see myself as a rapist, even when I saw a woman struggling, spread-eagled and tied down."

"How would you define a rapist, then?" Sally interjects.

His eyes take a quick survey of the room. "My idea of a rapist

36

is a tree jumper—a guy that snatches a woman off the streets in dark alleys and in the parks. And he just takes it for ten to fifteen minutes until he gets his satisfaction. What I've done, they all got satisfaction."

"How do you know that?" Sally asks.

He grins. "Because they'd be there two or three hours."

"But they were tied down and had no other choice," I object.

Zeke shrugs indifferently. "They were enjoyin' it," he insists. "I was taking them from behind and from the front. They were blowing me."

"Where did they get their enjoyment from?" Sally asks.

"I think from the time period of my being there they was enjoyin' it. In all cases. They had to. There was no way possible they didn't. I'm sure of it. It's nothing that they said, and it's nothing that they did."

"What did they say when it was over?"

He scratches his head as he answers. "They said, 'I'm gonna call the police' or 'I'm gonna tell my husband' or 'I'm gonna kill you' or 'Don't hurt me, don't kill me. I'll do anything. I won't call the cops—just don't kill me.'"

"How did you react to their pleas for mercy?"

"I knocked them out. I didn't want to hear it. I just wanted them to shut up."

"Those kinds of pleas didn't turn you on?"

He leans forward in his seat. "No," he says adamantly. "That's the part that scared me. That's why I had to knock them out."

"Why did it scare you?"

"I never came in there with the intention to hurt them, and after I was satisfied, my revenge was satisfied. I was gettin' ready to leave. And when I'm leavin' and they're still tied down, they're tellin' me don't kill them. It would be blank to me. I remember one time this woman told me not to kill her. And when she did my anger grew. I did want to kill her at that time because she said it. She was the first one who said, 'Don't kill me.'" Zeke shakes his head disapprovingly. "And at that time I was lookin' at her. She's tied down. If she did decide to call the police or whatever, she could identify me. Yeah, why not? Why don't I kill her? But then, when I knocked her out and she's layin' there, I came to my senses. I said, 'You can't kill this woman. You didn't go to the Vietnam War because you didn't want to kill. Don't kill her.' I lost that feeling."

37

A momentary silence fills the cubicle. Then I ask Zeke what would have turned him off in terms of raping a woman.

He answers quickly. "If they said, 'I want it.'"

"Why would that have turned you off?"

"Because I wasn't in there for her to want it," he says irritably. "She turned me down. She said no from the beginning. That's why I have to take it. If she tells me, 'Yeah, I want it, hit me, bite me, smite me,' that would have turned me off real quick. I believe I would've killed her or find another woman who wouldn't go through the ordeal I put her through."

"Did raping satisfy you sexually?" Sally asks.

He chuckles. "It felt good. Yeah, that's one of them. I got one of them. I thought, 'I got you back, Shirley. I paid you back for what you did to me.' I'd be smiling. I'd be happy that I used a woman. I felt an overall happiness that she's still laying out there tied up on the bed, and she won't come around until a half an hour or so—or until somebody finds her."

"Which rape do you remember most vividly?"

Zeke rattles off the incident smoothly, his hands slicing the air for emphasis. "There was a woman I met at the racetrack. She had a real chic outfit on, a clinging dress that was green. And I'd say her ass was as wide as that window." He points to the barred panes located just behind him.

"I was up on the sixth landing, and she was down by the fence. She must have had a filly in the race or something like that. I would look at her from behind, and she looked very pleasing to me. There was no possible way I could've talked to that woman. There were so many people around her. She used to call somebody, and when she did, she'd turn all the way around. And her body was like a model's. Her back was just fantastic. I seen her, and she left in a Rolls-Royce. So I figured she lived somewhere out on Long Island.

"So I followed her up to her house, and I seen that she had about three kids—unless one of them was her grandson. I seen two couples leave the house, so I figured that was my time to go in there. But something told me no, there's still someone in there. So I waited a little longer, and a man came out. She kissed him at the doorway, and I'd seen him—he was checking his watch. They was speakin'. He got into the car, and she went back into the house.

"Now, the house set off the road a good sixty feet, and she had trees in the front part of the house. I was standin' by one of the

38

trees noticing all this. So when she was goin' back into the house and the car was comin' down the driveway, I worked my way up the side of the house and I wound my way into the back door. I didn't have to use no window or anything—just creep my way through the back door. So I got into the house, and I'm down on the first landin' and comin' through. I come through a dining room, and I hear a voice. The voice is calling somebody. At that particular time, being that I'm in the dining room, the voice seemed like it was in the next room. I hid under the table." Zeke pauses, as if for dramatic effect.

"At that time I was scared. I didn't know what I was going to do—whether I was going to kill this woman or not. Is there a maid in here, or was that her boyfriend or her son? Maybe her husband was still there and I would have to fight. The noise of her calling stopped, and I creeped my way into the living room. I got behind this sofa chair, and I heard the door slam, and I heard her—which I didn't know at the time—coming down the stairs. Still, I'm not near any window. I'm not moving either. I'm waiting to see if there's anybody else in the house.

"She comes into the room, she picks up a book that was on the vanity, and she goes back upstairs. Now I waited for two minutes so I could hear if there was anybody else in the house. And I followed the stairway up, and I don't know which room it was. Now I had to search the rooms, and I searched two rooms before I found her in the room which as soon as I opened the door she screamed."

Zeke pauses to take a drag on his cigarette and exhales a thin stream of smoke. I silently marvel at the detail in which he can recall this incident. It's as if it had happened only yesterday instead of more than eight years ago.

"She threw the book at me—the one she was reading. Then she came up to me with a pair of scissors. And I knocked her around the room. I don't remember if I bruised her that bad, but I do remember hitting her repeatedly on the face. She was the most fightingest woman. She gave me a big fight. I hit her with a closed hand, and she hit the back of the bed." He makes a fist. "She had one of those sturdy beds. I never did want it on the bed, so I tied her to the floor—to the bottom of the bed—and I went from there." Zeke falls into a reflective silence.

"I took her the right way first, then she gave me some head, and then I had to turn her over. I told her I wasn't going to let her go until I'm satisfied. And she told me she did satisfy me. I said,

39

'No, that was only one time.' She told me her husband was coming back and her daughter was coming.

"We're up on the second floor, and as I was entering her from the back—and I just did about penetrate her—that's when I heard a car comin'. That's when I had to get out. And I just got out in time, because as I was goin' through the kitchen, I heard the front door close. So I had to go all the way to the front of that lawn and come all the way around to get away. That was the time somebody almost caught me." There's a grin on Zeke's face as he finishes his story.

"How were you arrested?" Sally asks.

"I was arrested by word of mouth. That rape right there was the attempted rape I'm in for. She said it was attempted rape. I guess she didn't want to say she was raped.

"I was in upstate New York trying to bail my brother out, who was in on drug charges. When I was doing that, this detective from the rape tactics squad of New Rochelle had a warrant for me. When they was doing that, the cops in Manhattan also had a warrant for me on narcotics. And being that narcotics is a more powerful charge than rape—mainly attempted rape—they pushed the rape charge on the side and got me with the drug charge."

"How did they get a description of you?"

He blows smoke into the air before answering. "They got me through a car. At that time I had a Mark IV. And I believe it was the husband or the daughter—whoever came into the house—that noticed the car. And I didn't think at that time it would be noticeable because there were Cadillacs, Rolls-Royces, all up and down that street."

"Would you like to meet any of your victims again?" Sally asks.

"Yeah, all of them," he grins.

"What would you say to them?"

This time Zeke giggles. "Let's do it again, that's what I'd say. Let's do it again."

"You mean you'd want to rape them again—you have no remorse?"

He shrugs. "No, why should I? Why should I regret it? They was all asking for it. They'd flaunt themselves. And if I wasn't in the position to do it, somebody else would. I got my satisfaction not out of raping them but by sodomizing them. That was my satisfaction—to take them in the back."

40

"That's bullshit. You raped them," I say.

"I'm not a rapist, I'm a sodomizer," he replies stubbornly. "I was like a specialist in what I was looking for in terms of sexual gratification."

Sally asks Zeke if he ever tried to rape the same woman twice. He shakes his head no.

"But you just said they enjoyed what you did to them, so why didn't you go back?"

He shifts uncomfortably in his chair. "One of the reasons I didn't go back is that I didn't want them to recognize me that I did it before," he tells Sally. "I'd like to see them again, though."

I change the subject and ask Zeke how he is treated by other inmates and by the guards.

"They call me Ice Cream in here," he says smoothly. "I got that name from some kids I met in Chicago and Saint Louis. In here they just put power on me. I got a good crew—that's eighteen hundred inmates. I could call close to fifteen hundred of them to carry my bags and throw down on someone in a given situation. No one messes with me. The officers, the majority you got in here are brand-new, kids that come out of high school. They don't know about jailhouse rules—that there's inmates in here, people in green, that's entitled to respect."

"Have you had any psychiatric treatment?" Sally asks.

He nods. "On my own, 'cause I kinda got scared one time because I was goin' to get married. And this girl heard I used to sodomize women, and she said that being I wanted to marry her, to get some psychiatric help. I visited a doctor for eight months. He just took my money, and he didn't help me. I had to help myself by talking it out, explaining the type of things I went through as I explained it today."

I glance at my watch; our time is almost up. There are one or two more questions I want to ask before Zeke leaves.

"When do you get out?"

He gives us his gap-toothed smile. "This year."

"Are you going to end up doing the same thing?"

"I might," he says matter-of-factly. "I won't say I'll never tie a woman down. I might do it. I might do it again. There's no tellin'."

Zeke adds an afterthought. "I'm looking at television now. These women on the disco shows they have, they're very appealing. The way they dress, the way they flaunt themselves. I see

41

myself sometimes at night—I tried my best, I held out five years—whipping myself, masturbating. And every time I see these disco shows, I go back to my cell and masturbate."

"What are your masturbatory fantasies?" Sally asks.

He fiddles with the ashtray. "I think of how I would do it with these women. Would I tie her up? And being that I'm looking at these magazines with sadomasochism, bondage, I believe that's my thing. As far as tying a woman down to a chair, bed, anything—to have her tied up and have her say no to me, that's my thrill."

I interrupt. "You really haven't learned a lesson from being arrested?"

He laughs bitterly. "I'm not comin' back in here. I have a plan. As I said, I ran a photography and filmmaking studio. I'm going into pornography. I'll probably deal with sadomasochism and rape. That's where my head is at as far as going out of here."

There's a brief pause before Sally asks the next question. "If you do rape again, you'll kill the woman so she can't give the police a description of you—right?"

Zeke locks eyes with her for a few moments. "Yeah. I don't ever consider myself ever living this hell again. This is my first time, and for me to come back again it would have to be for murder. Murder of who I have no thought of yet, but that would be the charge. But to ascertain that thought at this time—I don't see myself as a murderer."

I ask Zeke whether he believes he is sick and in need of psychiatric care.

"No, I don't think I'm sick," he says sharply. "Look at all the freaky things happenin' out there. There's people making love in discotheques, exhibitionists, people making love on trains and things. *That's* sick. People that likes to be watched by hundreds and thousands of people—those people are sick.

"What I do and what I've done as far as these women are concerned is undercover. They wasn't into bondage, they wasn't into anal sex, and I just introduced it to them. That's the way I see it. For me to go into it again, that's the way that I'll probably see it again. Just introducing them into another way of having sex. Being that they're virgin back there, they're no longer virgin after that."

"So you weren't raping women, you were instructing them?" I ask.

"Yeah, I believe I was," he says defensively. "I don't see no sickness in that."

Sally has one final question. "Do you really think any of the women you raped reached orgasm?"

He nods. "Yeah, all of them in one way or another. They had to. I satisfied them."

I tell Zeke our time is up.

"Man, those questions were tough," he says.

"So were some of your answers."

He smiles. "Just put down in your book I was a sodomizer—not a rapist. That was my specialty . . ."

Julio, age 24, was sentenced to five to ten years for forcible rape, kidnapping in the first degree and sodomy in the first degree. He served six years at Green Haven Correctional Facility and went for a parole hearing in 1980. He was denied parole and is now serving time at Otisville Correctional Facility.

"To know that she didn't want it, refused it, and then in the ultimate accepted it, enjoyed it—that fascinated me a lot."

Julio is decked out in his fanciest civilian clothes. He looks dapper in a green sweater, stylish pants, rose-tinted sunglasses, and a silver bracelet ominously embossed with skull and crossbones. He is a handsome guy with dark, curly hair cut short, a neatly trimmed mustache, and a history of rape that goes back to when he was fourteen.

I lead off with the usual question about background.

"I was born and raised on the Lower East Side of New York," Julio replies. "I was brought up like people in most underprivileged families who live in the ghetto—struggling to survive. You had to be strong, because most of the weak fall by the wayside. So I

45

started burglary, robberies, gang fights—that resulted in drugs. I started using amphetamines, drinking alcohol. I got hooked and from there started going to various drug programs.

"We were a family of four. I have a brother; he also went through the same. I also attended school. I went all the way to about the tenth grade. My school was good. I always enjoyed that. Because of conditions—family problems—that made me change my course of life."

"What kind of family problems?"

"My father was an alcoholic. He came down with cirrhosis of the liver. After he'd been drinking there'd be a lot of arguments in the family. Of course my family was very strict. They didn't understand us kids because we was young and had the desire to explore things like drugs. It caused a break in the family. The family broke up and left me without a home. So I slept in certain places with friends, and there were times when I didn't have anyplace to sleep at all. I had no other choice but to resort to crime to survive—just to be able to eat. I had several arrests for possession of narcotics, a few burglaries, robberies."

"How old were you when you left home?"

"I was eleven," he says, exhaling cigarette smoke. "I've been on my own ever since then. I haven't lived with my family since I was eleven years old. Even to this day I'm not in contact with them. I don't know where they are. They tried the best they could, but it was always something beyond their control—I had to leave."

"How old were you when you committed your first rape?"

He stops to think for a moment. "Fourteen or fifteen."

"Tell us about it."

He pats his hair nervously. "You see what happened, because I had no home, had no family, I used to go into the metropolitan cities. And most of these cities, they had like peep shows, massage parlors, prostitutes. I found the only possible ways of me maintaining income would be for me to reside in those cities, because the opportunities are greater in terms of money.

"While stayin' down there I'd frequent a lot of bars, and I met an old fella. He took a liking to me. He started tellin' me it would be good for me to be a pimp because I'd be able to maintain money. At that age I was young, and I didn't understand it. I'd seen him gettin' money, so I was after the same thing. I became what you refer to as a pimp. So that started my exploits of women."

Julio nervously crushes out his cigarette. I make a mental note that he is one of several rapists we've already interviewed who were at one time pimps.

"This old man, he told me one of the best ways to maintain women was to seduce them and rape them. Take them into small rooms and things like that and let them stay for long periods of time—to forcefully introduce sexual intercourse as a means for them to submit. So I continued to do this. After, I'd say, about eight months, I found a different change in my personality. It wasn't so much that I was in it for the game or the enjoyment of the game. I found that I actually liked it when I'd force a woman to have sexual intercourse.

"To this day here," Julio concludes, spitting the words out in rapid little bursts, "I think I got a pretty clear picture of the things that motivated me. I feel very infatuated just watching those cunts' facial features—the contours of her face when I'm forcefully taking her rather than having her grab me and say, 'Hey, I'm hot. I want to have sexual intercourse.' I feel very fascinated just to watch facial features, the contours of the face. This is what turned me on."

"Did you feel powerful and in charge when you were raping a woman?" Sally asks.

Julio shrugs indifferently. "It wasn't a machismo, chauvinistic type of thing. I just enjoyed the fact that it was done by force, and I liked to notice the expressions on their face. I felt that just certain ways that their face was patterned in the process of screwing, that they were submitting and enjoying it—it excited me."

"How did you get these women?"

He grins. "I always had this talent to attract women. I found that easy. Most women would come to me because of my appearance. I'd always dress well. They were attracted to me, fascinated by me. Because I'd always go into a bar or a disco or something, and it was just like a magnet. A lot of the time I was attracted to them as well. It was no problem.

"Like I'd take them to the apartment, and I'd know that she was going to consent to the fact anyway," he says with unrestrained braggadocio. "I wouldn't wait for the consent. I'd do it deliberately—the forceful act. They found that very strange. A lot of them didn't press no charges. They'd see me even after that, and they'd think that I was weird. They just couldn't understand it. But a lot of them just didn't press charges because they figured they wanted it anyway—but 'Why did he do it by force?' is the question that constantly puzzled them." Julio smiles at the memory.

Sally asks the next question. "How many women did you rape?"

"Two. One of them, she was fifteen—I know she was fifteen. I knew her from the Bronx when I used to live in the Bronx. I had had sex with her prior. It was willing. This time I was a little drunk or high, and I had took her to my apartment, and I supposedly raped her." He pauses to light another cigarette.

"But again, she didn't want to press charges. But she went home to her mother and all that, and she eventually did. So she did what she was instructed to do. She was a runaway, and if she didn't do that, her mother would have had her put away. I was arrested for it, but they gave me a few misdemeanors—endangering the welfare of a child. They gave a lie detector test and found out she was lying."

"Which rape charge got you convicted?"

He exhales a cloud of smoke before replying. "She was a Caucasian lady. I happened to know her back when. She was with me for about a year. This could be one of her fetishes as well, but she enjoyed it when I first did it. She found it kind of strange. She was crying and things like that.

"In a lot of these cases I didn't use physical abuse. There may have been periodically—times like when I was high. Well, like when I first raped her she was shocked and she was just dazzled. She didn't know what was what. And at this time I had tied her to the bedpost. This was the first time, and she disapproved of it and everything. And even after that, other times, she would just welcome it and just request that I do it in this manner. Somehow she just got to like it.

"And what happened after that is that I had made contact with other ladies, and like I said, I always had the magnet to attract. And I guess she became overly jealous and she finally said that about me—that I raped her. She pressed charges."

"Did you always get into bondage when you raped?" I ask.

He smiles broadly. "No, not always. In fact, I just got that out of *Penthouse* magazine. I never knew about that until I read that magazine."

"Did you do anything more bizarre than bondage?"

Julio's face becomes animated, and he gestures elaborately as he answers. "I enjoyed sodomizing. I guess it was a thrill that"—he searches for the right words—"I guess that I somehow felt a lot of times that when I had sexual intercourse with a woman in her cunt,

48

it didn't cause the kind of expressions that I wanted to see on her face.

"I don't think it was a feeling of superiority. I always enjoyed seeing the expression on a woman's face. I don't know, it just excited me, the manner in which she did it. The thing I found was that I just liked to admire the body. There may be times when I may tell her just to lie on her stomach, and I'd just feel and observe a lady for a half-hour, forty-five minutes, and she found it strange. I may touch her on a certain part of her body for an hour or two. They all found that strange, but I guess they ultimately all got accustomed to it. They enjoyed the manner in which it was done."

"You did all this and then you raped them?"

He shakes his head affirmatively.

"Why?"

"To give them pleasure," he replies, as though the answer is obvious.

"Did you ever use a weapon?"

He nods. "You see, I've always carried a knife. If I didn't carry that I'd carry a gun. That was a means of protection for the type of life I was leading. Even as a child I always carried a gun. There was never a time where I had trouble with her where I had to use a knife or any type of force."

Sally asks Julio what he did to keep his victims from violently struggling.

He thinks for a moment. "I'd be screaming or imposing fear in that fashion by using vulgarity or something. Most of them would succumb just to the fact that I was yelling or that I used words very harshly."

"I still don't understand about those facial expressions. Tell me more," I say.

"You see, I was looking for just their expressions—not in the case where I was trying to seduce her or wrestling or tussling with her, but just during intercourse itself. Just the fact that she wouldn't submit and just seeing the expression. Another thing that fascinated me, you see, is that when we were screwing, she had like a frown on her—a frown on top of an attitude of 'Well, I hate you.' You could see all the animosity on her face."

He pauses. "And then, after awhile, during the process of having intercourse the frown leaves. It becomes submission, willingness—and sometimes even a smile under a certain fantasy she would see in reaching the orgasm. And to know that she didn't

49

want it, refused it, and then in the ultimate accepted it, enjoyed it—that fascinated me a lot."

"When their faces changed, did that make you feel more like a man?" Sally asks.

Julio gives her a half-smile. "I don't know if I would say that. I've always known I was a man. I come up being a man. Some people's definition of being a man is to work nine to five, support a wife, have children. Others' is to let nobody disrespect them, whatever it may be. I always thought myself a man. It wasn't something that I was searching for, the me that was not. It was just the excitement of the face."

"Where do you think you got the need to be excited in this way?"

He ponders the question for a moment, toying with a book of matches. "Mine stems back from the day I met that old fella. He was a pimp. I worshiped him more or less because I started receiving a lot of money by listening to him. And being so young I continued this when I got arrested for some small cases of drugs and came back. Somehow the way he used to explain it—he used to demonstrate a lot of times. Like he'd have maybe five or six women in the house, and he would call me over, call me Youngblood." Julio smiles at the recollection.

"Like I would just sit there and watch him. Like he would have them all strip his clothes before sexual intercourse, lesbian acts, and whatever. And just the manner in which he was doing it—he would tell me things he liked, certain expressions he'd like to see. And he always knew how to explain it. Just the way you're thinking about it or see it, he was able to explain it. I would say I attribute it most to the fetishes he had. But because he was much older, much more intuitive than I was, mine resulted in this type of action."

"Did you ever go walking down the streets looking for a woman to rape?"

Julio nods vigorously. "Many times. There was a time when I took a train ride, you know, and I caught myself at this time in the process of recruitin' women. And I would sit down in the train, and I would see a lady—you know, her legs is crossed—and I would look at her face. It wasn't so much the legs or anything else that excited me. It pertains to age—young, old, even babies sometimes, that crossed my mind." Julio folds his hands on his lap and tries to read Sally's reaction.

"Normally, it's always a face. I would look at a face and imagine what kind of expressions she would give me. Would it be like Susan's, or would it be like Maria's?—and I compared it with them. And I started drawing my own conclusions, right? And then I wanted to actualize it. And I would just want it to remain like that. I would sit right next to her, and if there wasn't a seat available, maybe I'd drop a dollar or something like that. I'd say, 'Excuse me, is this dollar yours?' Just a means of getting into her, you know. Or I would say, 'Excuse me, I'm reading this here book, and I'm having trouble understanding this word. Could you help me?' Anything so you can get a response so you can introduce.

"Like, most times it worked. When it didn't work for a particular one I wanted, I would get aggravated. I would pursue her wherever she would go. But a lot of times I was drawn off that because a lot of times the police would be there with their cars passing. So I'd forget all about it.

"There was one case in particular—I met one by the subway, and I looked at her. You see, actually, being around women for so long, I developed a thing where I could more or less look at a woman and tell what sort of characteristics—what's her nature, what's she composed of. And a lot of times on the subway I'd seen one, and I gave it a label already—she's a freak, which meant she's the type of woman that's easy. She's fair game, and she would do anything that's requested.

"I met one of those freaks, and although she wanted to give me, I didn't want to wait, because I was so hot in the pants and I thought I wanted to take it. Like I had threatened her with a knife, you know, but I wasn't going to use it. I just put my hand in my pocket, like if I had it out. And I took her to the apartment and everything. With her, like most others, I did it forcibly, but in the long run they got to like it.

"I questioned myself," he continues in a tone of deep sincerity. "Was it the fact that they consented to it after I reached orgasm? Was it the fact that my appearance—I can't exactly pinpoint it. But I'm trying to figure out to this day, was the fact that they enjoyed it at the end due to my makeup? Was it part of my appearance? I haven't really found the answer. I've stumbled over some things. I don't know in truth if that is what it is."

Sally asks if Julio believes all women have secret rape fantasies.

He grins at the question. "That's true, in my opinion. This is personal, a product of my own experience. Today even more so

51

because society is so highly sexed. Everywhere you go there's pornography. The mentality of the young is being infested by so much pornography."

Sally asks again how many women Julio raped.

"It comes out to about a total of eight," he answers, upping his previous estimate considerably.

"Did you ever rape them anywhere else but in apartments?"

"Mostly apartments," he says curtly.

"Did you ever grab them and drag them into alleys?"

He shakes his head sideways and lights a cigarette, inhaling pleasurably.

"You said you enjoyed sodomizing, right?"

Julio smiles. "Yeah, I enjoyed that. I always had that desire to sodomize because that was one of the things I was influenced by the old man. When I met him he always told me it was always good to sodomize women, because when you have sexual intercourse with them in the vagina, they may not feel it.

"You know, you may not have a penis large enough or something. But the old man says if you want to be a good pimp, you always got to sodomize them. So in one case you won't have no babies and her attention will always be solely directed to you. In another case it would hurt her, afflict her, and she would feel something towards this. So I did it. I lived under the principle. I got to enjoy it."

I ask Julio, who seems lost in thought, whether he believes he is a sick person.

He mulls it over for a few seconds. "No, I felt confused," he finally answers. "The reason why I don't think myself sick is that most people that come out of pimping—and I've been in that life for years—most are classified as deranged, sick, because that's not the norms of society. It's not supposed to be like that. A life like that is automatically classified as sick."

Sally breaks in. "How do you define a rapist?"

Julio looks thoughtful. "I'd say there's degrees of rape. I've heard through the papers of a lot of cases about where the guy is extremely psychotic. He raped not just a woman but their sisters and mothers and then murdered them. Things like that I consider to be extreme. A case like that even I would say is sick."

I ask Julio whether he has ever been raped in prison.

"No," he says, "because I have a reputation."

"What kind of reputation?"

52

"Like, you see, in most prisons sometimes we have to demonstrate because there's people who have been in prison here for many years. When they came in prison everything was normal. But after being with men for so many years, why, you lose some of the masculine qualities." He scrutinizes my face.

"You tend to move more towards males because of the environment here. You know, they've been down ten, twelve, fifteen years, and they see somebody come in—they say, 'Hey, he look just like a woman.' He would be kind of attracted to that because he's been away from the opposite sex for so long. This would cause them to come at you. They bribe you, they help you out, and this puts you in an obliged position. But I never had no problems, because as soon as I came in I started very aggressively, whether it was the guards or an inmate—whatever it was. I did that deliberately, just to let them know if they come, be prepared. But don't come with no bribes. Come straight up." There is a hard expression on Julio's face.

"Do any of the other inmates know you're a rapist?"

"Some of them know. But in this penitentiary a rapist is classified as someone who's done something terribly immoral—like raping a mother or killing a family. This is what they consider rape. If you was around this penitentiary and ask inmates what they consider rape, in my opinion the statistics would come out that most of them consider that psychotic, extreme form of rape is rape. If I was to tell them about my case, they wouldn't view it as rape. They'd say that's one of the faults of the elements of life—of trying to be a pimp. They wouldn't perceive mine as a rape case.

"But if you spoke about a case where a family was involved, or a baby girl—like a lot of these guys raped girls eleven and twelve—when they hear about a rape like this they get angry. A lot of them also got the type of attitude that I got, although they might not have led the type of life I led."

"What do you mean?"

"They're the product of the same environment. And they feel in a lot of cases women put them up to that. They take them out or give them some kind of invitation for you to drive them over there—you know. They're up here for rape but don't really believe it's rape. They know they don't fall in that extreme category, no matter what the indictment papers say. They know it was just a thing where they wanted to come out for the evening and she didn't want to have intercourse with him. He thought that she was playing

53

with him, playing games with him. So in the final analysis he grabbed her, ripped her clothes off, and had sex with her. You know. There are cases here that are like that."

Sally asks how Julio feels about women in general.

He smiles at her. "I have two babes who come up here and visit me now. My attitude has changed completely. The nature of a woman in my opinion is to produce—production, procreate, extension of the family. My attitude now is that I don't think I'm superior. I'm not scornful. I understand now that they have their own opinions, their own attitudes about certain things. I appreciate the differences because I think that I grow behind that. But there was a time where I couldn't be comfortable with a woman and just sit down and speak with her, because I always thought I was better than they are. The way I was influenced, the pimp was always better than the woman. At no time did he show weakness.

"I can say that now I can cry—now when I speak to a woman I can show them my real side. At one time I couldn't do that. I had that barrier. They was always wrong. Today they have a voice with me—not so much because of women's liberation, but I found out just being yourself, I'm growing even today. That'll never stop."

"You say you stalked women on subways and that at first you would approach them?" Sally asks.

He nods.

"What would you advise women to do in this situation?"

Instead of answering, Julio launches into a description of the way he operated. "I had contrived several techniques like the dollar. I would never ask them for a match, because I found that to be outdated at that time. Everybody else used that, you know. I would do certain things, like I would have a camera and I would take a picture of her. I would put it in an envelope and pass by, and I would drop the picture. I'd say, 'Is this picture yours?' And she was completely dazzled because she didn't see me taking any picture and she didn't know where it came from. I knew the mere fact that she had never took one, this would compel her to talk," he continues. "And all I wanted then was for her to say something. That would give me an in as a means to raping her. From there I would simply talk about the photo and ask her her name."

"But what would have turned you off?" Sally interrupts.

He hunches his shoulders. "I don't know. I've never been asked that question, but it's food for thought. The way the cosmetic world is today, the way the fashions is, you have to talk. They look very

54

good, they're luscious, they're gorgeous, desirable—you know."
Julio locks eyes with me. I shrug noncommittally.

"And you know, when you see them, I say to myself, 'Can I pay that lady a compliment without seeming facetious, without flattering her?' I answered myself that I can because I'm very attractive."

He finally touches on Sally's original question. "A woman not saying anything to a rapist may turn him on—the fact that she just refuses. If she talks, then she'll say, 'Well, I've given him a lead. I'll open the doors for him to come through if I say anything.' It's very hard. Then again, all the women is the same in nature."

Sally ignores his vagueness and returns to her question about what would have turned him off. His voice seems edged with hostility when he replies.

"*Nothing*. It's like I've been trying to tell you, the influence of this person who brought me into this game, this life—they call it the game of life, right?" He pauses, as if waiting for some response. "He was very brilliant. There's no question. For deceptiveness he was very brilliant. He had shown me techniques where, for example, if I met a lady in the subway and seen that she smiled too much, this would now give me the impression that maybe she's police, undercover agent or somethin'. I would hold off. That might deter me, but nothing would deter me if she spoke or didn't speak.

"I've noticed that they got a kind of spray now, and some are given to studying in karate school. I guess all of them are elements to prevent it. I'd like to give some better suggestions, but I don't have none. Sprays, guns, karate I think is good."

"Would you want to meet your victims again?" Sally asks.

He replies quickly. "Yes, I would want to apologize. I tried to get in contact with one, but to no avail. But I would apologize. I was terribly wrong. And I wouldn't be ashamed of it or nothing. I was thinking of sending her flowers."

Julio looks thoughtful for a moment. Then he continues. "If I hadn't been stopped the way I was that day, I might have winded up killin' somebody. There's no tellin', because the time that I got arrested was the time I was raping very strong. One of them might have had a gun or something. One of them might have killed me, or I might have had to kill them."

"Did you think of killing any of the women you raped?"
He shakes his head no.
"Bondage was as far as you went?"

55

"Yeah, and I learned that from *Playboy* magazine."
"What kind of scars did this leave on you?"

"I just met a young lady that went to Hunter College," he replies. "I don't want to tell her that I had raped, but I don't want to lie. So eventually I have to. But what effects will it have? . . . None. I'd like to apologize if that would do anything. I wish it had never happened like this, but it don't leave no scars because I'm getting better inside on who I am now. I realize that that was one of those transient stages of my life I was living in. I had no mind. I was very easily influenced. Sex, you know, excited me. I learned the fetishes that he liked. I found out why he enjoyed them, so I wanted to enjoy them."

I signal to Sally that our time is almost up. There is one more question she wants to ask. "Could you have an orgasm without raping a woman?"

Julio looks amused. "I never had problems with that. Like I've always come into contact with women. But it's just that certain manner of seeing it—the facial features, the frowns, the animosity turning to joy. Things like that turned me on."

"Anything else you want to add?"

"Yeah. The sprays, the guns, the karate schools—that's good for women to prevent it. . . ."

Sal, age 36, was charged with murder and attempted murder and was given twenty-five years to life at Green Haven Correctional Facility. He has currently served ten years and is eligible for parole in 1999.

"I found more satisfaction when the girl is completely out. You can take more advantage of her, get all the pleasures you want. Later on . . . I killed them even before I fucked them."

A tall, stocky man wearily enters the room and helps himself to a seat. He is wearing a green shirt and brown pants. His oily black hair is slicked back. Thick eyebrows perch over deeply set eyes that seem to have a vague expression. An angular nose juts out from unshaven cheeks.

We introduce ourselves to Sal, and he shakes my hand with a loose grip, as if he doesn't want to touch me. He fixes an intense stare on Sally, who nervously lights up a cigarette. I recall uneasily the letters he wrote agreeing to be interviewed. The childish hand-writing, the chilling tone.

Sally breaks the uncomfortable silence. "Tell us something about your background."

"I was born in New York City. I was the oldest of three kids in the family." Sal answers questions in a sluggish monotone. He has a thick New York accent, and his voice is a sound-alike for Bogart's. He punctuates his remarks with a flick of his right thumb. "I went to junior high school, that's all. I was raised a Catholic, but I didn't like it, so I changed my creed to Jewish."

"Why Jewish?"

"I find Jewish more satisfying. I used to believe in Jesus Christ, but he only stands for one thing, and he had no power over the Almighty. So I disbelieve him because God is a little more bigger. I like the faith. I like the Jewish faith. I converted in Attica State Prison."

"How did you get along with your mother?" Sally asks.

He takes a long drag on his cigarette. "I was always close to my mother—not my father."

"How did she treat you?"

Sal frowns. "Well, if I got into trouble as a kid, I'd get it from the back hand—that was from my father, not my mother. My sisters get into trouble, I get the blame for it. I don't get along with my father. My case—the murders—that involves a lot of things. It involves why did I do it. I've been told by psychologists—their findings of talking to me—that it all involves my father. Because when I was fourteen years old I had a bad experience with my father. You want to know exactly?"

"Yes, if you want to tell us."

"First I went out looking for my younger sister." Sal has a habit of beginning sentences in the middle of nowhere. "I didn't find her, and she showed up. I was laying in the bed, and my father, he had a knife, a Boy Scout knife—what I always carry. Fortunately it wasn't open, but he threw it at me. He hit me right in the balls and put me in the hospital for a few weeks. I always got a fear from him concerning that. He's a drinking man, and he gets violent when he drinks. If you're not home on time—even for a fellow—you can always tell if he's going to become outrageous and start swinging. And I had a fear from that."

He changes the subject abruptly. "But considering my case itself, I have a little rejection of girls. When I was younger, every time I go out with a girl—which was not too frequent—every time I try to touch a girl, she denies it. I never did get along with you

58

females—*sex!*" He is staring at Sally, an amused grin on his face. "So I got a little thing about sex. I try to take it without them knowing it. So I find ways of getting it. It worked out pretty good for a time in my younger life, but I guess it grown on me. It came up in my earlier thirties. You do something as often enough as raping girls when you're younger, it's going to grow on you. It's hard to break it. I'm not too—how would you say it?—understanding." Sal smiles, evidently pleased with his choice of words.

"I always had one thing in my mind when I was younger—take advantage. You can't get it voluntarily, you have to take it. So I went around lookin' through windows. I started rapin' when I was fifteen. I used to find the girls. Normally they're very sexual-looking, young as my own age." He falls silent for a moment.

"You know, it's a very odd thing when you look through a window at a girl laying down and no one's there but you and her. You can take advantage of her because no one else is in the room. You get a sort of satisfaction, as if you were going to a room by yourself and coming out with relief—jerking off. Well, when you jerk off enough, you get tired doing that."

"Then what happens?" I ask.

He grins again. "You go out and rape," he answers, as though addressing the village idiot.

"What kinds of things do you think of when you jerk off?" Sally asks.

"I usually look at pictures or memories of girls I had previously seen through the windows."

"Do you think of having sex with them in any particular way?"

"Yeah, in a lot of ways. Usually I tied them down. I do everything I can do to them. Not to kill them, just to rape them. But that was my younger life. I got to despise them. By despising them, you get a girl that doesn't want it, and you despise girls, so you try and take it away from them. But if you take it from one girl, I found that in certain conditions I enjoy killin' them. That was in my later days. I think it started when I first raped a girl."

Sal falls into a momentary silence broken only by the whirring of the tape recorder. Outside the interview room, the gate clangs discordantly as prisoners and their visitors enter and leave the reception area.

"Can you talk more specifically about that first rape?"

"You mean, how did it come about? Well, when I wanted to rape a girl, the first time I tried it, it took me about a week to do it.

I was fifteen. First I had to find a girl. The school I was going to was a public school. So I had to pick out a girl that was good-looking enough to make me hot. So you had to know where she gets off of school, where she goes—I had to follow her—where she lives, if she's on the first floor or the second floor. Usually the second floor is pretty hard to get to. You had to use a ladder, you know? The main floor is different if it's a two-family house.

"The first girl I raped, I find out by following her that she's on the first floor and has her own room. And I finally got to the point after watching her for almost a week, taking her clothes off, going to sleep . . . this particular girl, she just takes her clothes off and goes to sleep. She doesn't put anything else on, like pajamas or a nightgown." Sal pauses. "As I was doin' it, I just kept lookin' at the body, not the face. I always tried to figure out how I would go about doin' it." He seems to fall into a reverie.

"How did you go about doing it?"

"I ended up trying to tie her down."

"How did you get into the house?"

"It was the main floor, and I went through the window. It was partially open anyway. I opened the window, I entered it, and the first thing I did was grab her mouth. She woke, and the first thing after that I hit her—I would say on the right side of the face—in the purpose of knocking her out. So I knocked her out, took her hands, tied them down, tied the legs down.

"Now I find myself in a room with her tied down. It's mostly involved to touch a girl, even after you tied her down. Because you keep looking, as I was—you keep looking at the body. She was young enough where she had a very tempting body."

"You mean you just stood there and looked at her?"

"Yeah, at least an hour or so, I think. She was knocked out, she didn't come to. When I saw her then start moving, it means she was coming to. So I put something in her mouth and tied it around her head so she wouldn't scream. I watched her even when she was awake. Now I started taking all my clothes off. I guess I was waitin' for what kind of reaction would she have if I take my clothes off. Because if I took off my clothes she'd realize I was going to rape her."

"What reaction did she have?"

"She was nervous, sweating, trying to pull loose."

"Did that turn you on?"

"Sure. It turned me harder."

60

"Was it at this point that you raped her?"

"Oh, I did it very slowly. I was new at it, so I started just touching her. She kept on moving, moving. That's driving me to what I planned to do. But when you plan something, it's hard to do it for the first time."

"Was she in pain at all?"

"She was most likely in pain because . . . because, well, blood was coming out of her."

There is a shocked silence in the room.

"Did you enjoy all that?" Sally finally asks.

Another grin. "Only when she was twisting her top part—her tits going back and forth." He motions illustratively. "That got me hotter. I didn't want to stop. I just kept fucking her. The next minute I knew, I was looking out the window from where I was on her. It was daylight. I knew I was there, oh, about eleven at night, because she used to go to bed at ten o'clock. So I must have been fucking her all night. What she was doing made me fuck her more— the way she struggled."

"What were your thoughts immediately afterwards? Was it a letdown, or what?"

"When I saw it was daylight, I said to myself, 'I have to get out of here.' I get outside the window, I look in, she's still immobile. Well, I achieved what I wanted to do. I took it from a girl. But I said to myself that I didn't like it."

I look at him skeptically.

"I didn't like it," he repeats sullenly. "'Sal,' I said to myself, 'you just took it from a girl. She's laid down. You tied her down and you took it from her.' And I felt sorry for her because she can't move. She tried to fight me with her hands and legs. I felt sorry for her."

I remain unconvinced. "How many women did you rape?"

He ponders. "It must have been in the hundreds," he says matter-of-factly. The figure is staggering, as is his answer to my next question.

"How many of them did you murder?"

"Twenty-five," Sal replies without hesitation.

"Tell us about the first murder."

"I didn't plan nothing. To kill a girl, you don't actually plan it. It just happens that way. I saw her from a distance, her and her girlfriends. I followed her one day, and she walked to the beach. I waited to find out what kind of girl she was, what she really looks

61

like. You can't see far enough with her clothes on unless she's a really sexy girl, you know? So I said to myself, 'I want her.' So I went and got her. I went through the window, but unfortunately, just like the rest of them, they just resist you. And I slapped her too hard with my fist." He clenches his powerful hands as if to demonstrate.

"You hit her because she was struggling too hard?"

"She was struggling. Unfortunately I had a knife on me. When I was fucking her, she started waking up and started screaming. I stuck the knife in her chest to keep her quiet."

"Did you keep on raping her?"

"I didn't stop."

"You mean you kept on after you killed her?"

Sal simply shrugs.

"Did you get off on that?"

"Actually, seeing the blood come out of her, I didn't want to stop. I just kept fucking her. I didn't know she was dead. And all I said to myself, 'Well, she can't scream anymore.' I had all my pleasures. It was gettin' light, and I had to get out of there because I only lived around the corner." He falls into a reflective silence.

"Did you continue to rape and murder after that?"

"Yeah. I was twenty years old. I remember each time the blood came out of them it made me hotter. Mostly from the chest."

"Did you stab them all in the breast, then?"

"Anywhere I can, just to keep their hands away, to keep their mouth shut. I found more satisfaction when the girl is completely out. You can take more advantage of her, get all the pleasure you want. Later on, in the 1970s, I killed them even before I fucked them. I would stab them first, kill them, fuck them, and then beat the body with my fists."

"Would you have an orgasm as you beat them?" Sally asks.

"Oooh, I'll tell you. I can remember a lot of things about that. First of all, to hit a girl, to hurt a girl, you have to know exactly where to hit her. So I found fourteen ways of hitting her, and she'll be absolutely defenseless. So every time I see a girl alone down the street or something, entering a room, I make sure the girl is not there so that when she comes into the room I can hit her, bring her down to a size where I can take advantage of them. I would hit them, strip them, rip their clothes off, and stick them in front of a mirror. I'd hold their mouth and stick a knife in their chest while they were awake."

"You put them in front of a mirror?"

"Yeah, so they could see it."

"You put them in front of a mirror so they could watch themselves being murdered?" His words conjure up an image that stuns both of us.

"Yeah," he coolly replies.

"That made you sexually excited?"

"Yeah, that made me very hot—watching their reactions being stabbed or the breast cutting open."

"What made you so hard up that you had to murder to have an orgasm?" I ask.

Sal is unperturbed by the question. "To me it was worth it. Because every time I went to see a decent girl, she always refused me. So I took it upon myself to punish them."

"Did you always follow the same procedure?"

"In the beginning it was first stabbing them. That was three or four of them, I think. It was finding ways to render them to my own likings by hitting them in a certain place. And when that worked, whatever clothes they had on I'd take off. Sometimes I had to cut it off. Then I'd put them in front of a mirror, just hold their mouths and wait for their reactions. I'd slowly use a knife without even penetrating their skin. It just turned me on just doing it."

"What else did you do?"

"Three women, I used to tie their hands behind their back, put them in front of a mirror—one of those hall mirrors—tie 'em in such a way where she can't use her hands. I'd put her entire front, face and body, against the mirror, squeezing, touching, turning her around—all sorts of things like that." His hands massage an imaginary body as he speaks.

"Was there any special type of woman you were looking for?"

"Yes. Big tits. The bigger the better. When they're flat-chested they're not very sexy. I don't feel it's very sexy. It does not stimulate my feelings to them. The girls with the big tits are the most sexiest. They were what really turned me on, what would drive me to my wildest." Sal's face is twisted into a crooked grin.

"How were you arrested?"

"Well, they didn't find me at the scene of the crime. They took it for granted that I was the one that did it because of other rapes, but they couldn't really prove it. No weapon. They found a lot of knives, but no evidence to say this is the weapon that was

63

used in this particular case.

"Just two days after I did my little act—I was going to trade school in the morning at that time—I came out and I saw this police car going back and forth. He said I should come over there and give him an ID card. He asked if I saw any strange people around. I knew who he was talkin' about. They was lookin' for the rapist. I ain't gonna tell him. He's a cop. That same day, at night, two detectives come. Before I knew it I was in jail."

"How do the other inmates treat you?"

"I don't advertise as being a fag or anything like that. I'm a man that stays on his own. I get along with all the inmates, the guards. If you respect them, they'll respect you. It's a nice place to be, really. No trouble."

"How do you generally feel about women?" Sally asks.

"It's not like I used to exercise my feelings. Being in jail and knowing the fact what is a woman for, I see a woman is to have a life with—give life, not to take it. I find to understand a woman more is to get along with her, is to give her the kind of love a woman needs." He gives Sally a look of utmost sincerity. "It's like from the beginning and now. It's like teaching yourself not to think and not to feel the way I used to feel. I'm realizing in jail what it means to take a life. By changing my outlook of creed and being a Jew, it gives me more understanding about women."

"What kind of understanding?"

"They should be cared for, understand them, give them a lot of love if you have one. Unfortunately I don't have any."

"Do you feel any remorse about all the women you raped and murdered?"

"I feel sorry. As I learned more about women, it was the wrong thing to do. It was the wrong thing to feel. Right now, since I've been to jail, I've been trying to—and so far succeeding—to lose the habit of taking it all the time."

"What really set you off to rape?"

"It was to break the habit of masturbating. I had chances of looking at a girl, I wanted it from her. That kind drove me to it. I wanted her if she didn't give it to me. I got so mad I wanted to take it."

"You mean you felt it was your right to take it from her?"

"Of course it was my right. I felt that way. I figure if you're not going to give it to me, then it's my right to take it. So I took it any way I can." Sal seems disturbed by the question and stubs his cigarette out energetically.

"When you masturbate now, what kind of fantasies do you have?" Sally asks.

He smiles. "The pictures I got on my wall, that's the only thing that turns me on. Or when you look at a blank wall, you can see a lot—what your past is. You see women, you see girls, and you find things in a girl you can turn on. I have a lot of photographs of naked women and women with clothes on. I can look at a girl—and not even looking at that girl, just looking at someone—and they'd remind me of someone I'd known before."

"Do you ever masturbate thinking about the women you raped and murdered?"

He nods vigorously. "I get satisfaction coming that way. You see, you can't actually touch a girl in here. You can't have access of touching another girl. If I did, what I know now, I would be very hesitant to touch her, even touch her hand. Not because of the punishment—it's just the question of taking advantage of a woman anymore. I'd like a woman to take advantage of me whenever she can. But unfortunately there's not that many women to take advantage of me." He sighs and lights another cigarette. "I always think back to the women I raped, because they always gave me that stimulation. It still gives me stimulation."

"Do you think of yourself as a rapist?"

"No, I don't think of myself as a rapist. You might say it's crazy, but I think of myself as a lover of women. Because I had so many which I took from, and they still turn me on right now—even if they're dead or still walking around. In the condition I'm in now, you can't actually go out and get a girl the way you can when you're on the streets. You have to reduce your feelings to thinking about the women you took from. And that gives me as much satisfaction as doing it."

"What's the difference between a rapist and a lover?"

"A rapist is one that takes it all—has no limits, takes what he wants. He doesn't give a damn about the person he's taking it from."

"But that's exactly what you did."

"I'm just sayin' I'm not a rapist now because I've learned more about women not to be a rapist. I'm more of a lover right now because I have educated my mind, which I didn't when I was younger." He turns to Sally. "You know a lot of women. Maybe you can get one to write to me. I'd like to have a woman to express my feelings to, to tell them how I've changed."

Amos, age 27, was given ten to twenty-five years for rape in the first degree. He served six years of that sentence at Green Haven Correctional Facility and was conditionally released on April 17, 1979.

"I guess I was lonely and I wanted attention.
I wanted a mother image, right, 'cause
I hated my own mother—someone else I could
have loved 'cause she would have treated
me nice, spoiled me and did what I wanted her
to do."

Amos was an early starter, a kind of child prodigy. He was already having sexual encounters at age seven and committed his first rape when he was twelve. Before Amos was finally nailed, he had chalked up twenty or more rapes. Still, the young man who enters the visiting room hardly seems to fit the description of a hard-core rapist. He has a friendly, open manner that even his years in prison have failed to tarnish. He's wearing a black-and-brown sweater, and his face seems etched in a perpetual smile.

As he sips a cup of black coffee, Amos tells us he's a bit
nervous this morning. Not only is he due for release within a matter
of days, but shortly after he's done with this interview, he's sched-
uled to take his college exams. He says he intends to walk out of
Green Haven with a degree in his hands. We wish him luck.

"Tell us about your upbringing," Sally begins.

Amos begins to talk about his childhood. He says that he was
born into a poor family and raised in upstate New York. "I've been
involved with crime ever since the age of nine," he continues. "I
could say I'm used to being institutionalized to a certain extent,
because the majority of my youth years have been behind prison
walls. Also, I've been in state hospitals, shelters, and things of this
nature."

As Amos speaks, his hands flutter nervously, either clawing
the air or touching parts of his body. He also has a habit of constantly licking his lips.

"My family, uh, at this point in my life we don't actually
speak, and then we didn't even speak because of the fact that I
wanted to see life in my own aspect as they seen in theirs. And they
couldn't accept my standards, so therefore I went out and did what
I had to do in order to survive. And through surviving I took some
knocks and falls."

He smiles at us rather sheepishly before continuing. "Also my
first thing dealing with some type of sexual gratification with an
individual was in the house one day, and my mother, I think . . . I
think I did something spiteful because she did something to me. I
asked her for something, and she rejected me for it, and I took it
out on one of my sisters. I don't think the intent was there, my
need, because I was young and she was also young, right?"

I am confused. "You mean you molested your sister or something?"

"From playing around something did take effect," he says
vaguely. "As a result, I had to go upstate to reform school for that.
We were actually in the house alone, and I had a friend that came
up—he just came from training school in upstate New York. And,
uh, he was there, and he—you know—more or less started probin'
towards me to let him do somethin' with my sister."

Amos frowns at the memory. "I said, 'Get out of here. I'm not
goin' for that, you know.' So therefore I told him, I said, 'Look,
man, there's some other girls across the hall. If you want something, go over there, right?' And my sister, she more or less broke

into hysterics at this point, you know—like no one touched her, but she broke into hysterics. So I grabbed her to calm her down, right? And she came off calling, 'I want him, I want him,' like this here."

Amos now looks perplexed. "So I actually said, 'Well, go ahead,' you know. So when my mother came in, she had—well, you know—busted the whole setting up, right? She blew up. She got a knife, and she wanted to kill her family." He smiles wanly. "She wanted to do this, she wanted to do that, and I tried to restrain her, right? And we went to court, where she said my sister was raped, right? With me and this other individual. And the judge sent me up for a period of eighteen months."

Sally is not convinced by his story. "What did you really do to your sister?" she asks.

He avoids her eyes, fidgets with his hands, and generally appears extremely uncomfortable. He later admits that he has been treated for various nervous disorders since he was a kid. He also tells us that since he first went to reform school, he has appeared before no less than thirty-six psychiatrists, though in recent years he has had virtually no psychiatric care.

Sally is still waiting for an answer.

Amos shifts in his seat. "I raped her, I literally raped her," he replies in a quiet voice.

"Did she struggle?"

He nods. "It was a struggle. But then she just gave in and went along with it," he says, falling into a reflective silence. "I think overall why I raped my sister and continued to rape people was 'cause of the fact that I guess I was lonely and I wanted attention. I wanted a mother image, right, 'cause I hated my own mother—someone else I could have loved 'cause she would have treated me nice, spoiled me and did what I wanted her to do."

Amos folds his hands on his lap like a model pupil waiting for the teacher to ask him the next question. Sally obliges. "How did you get along with your parents?"

"I never did know my real father," he replies, tapping on his empty coffee cup. "At three weeks old I was found in the street. I was in a carriage, and a truck was supposedly coming towards me. I was in a state of shock. I was in a state of shock for a good month, and during that month nobody came to the hospital to claim me. The man who took me to the hospital, after a certain period of time he went to the authorities and took me in as his son. He raised me. I never met my mother until I was seven years old. I never met my immediate family until I was seven years old. I didn't even know I had brothers and sisters until I was seven, and when I found out I did have sisters and brothers . . ."

He pauses for a moment. "The way my aunt was treating them, it seemed as if something was tooken from me. Before that I was with the middle class. I was passin' grades with flyin' colors. I was a little genius at that time." He smiles bitterly.

"As soon as I met my immediate family, it seemed as if something was tooken from me. The gift that I was gifted with was drained from me because I was being humiliated. I was bein' beat by anything they could get their hands on, because I would rebel. I used to tell them, 'Don't hit me, talk to me.' I was very sarcastic and very open about how I felt. I dealt with my own feelings at that time. I think my uncle thought, 'I'm gonna have hell with this young man, so I'm gonna straighten him out now.'"

I interrupt to make sure I'm following him. "You mean you were reunited with your real family at age seven?"

He nods, explaining that the man who adopted him agreed to return him to his family. "I used to get beatings—for absolutely nothing. I seen my brothers get beatings with chickens—frozen chickens—like they were oriented to a down-South atmosphere, right? They brought it to New York, and comin' up in New York it's different. I mean, I don't know nothin' about no chickens and eggs and all this."

He grins and rubs the thin line of mustache that hugs his upper lip. "I'm exposed to the street gangs, I'm exposed to the slang of the street, the fast girls at school, the drugs—the whole scene. That's my world because that's what I chose. I felt I had friends in that world at that particular time. At that particular time I was also out for anything I could do to get attention from my mother. I guess the rapin' of my sister was to get my mother's attention."

"The other women you raped, was that a way of getting back at your mother—the way she hurt you?" Sally asks.

He looks thoughtful. "The women I raped, I had it in my mind that it was the image of my mother. The slightest little thing, the slightest little thing that triggered a nerve in me and a spark in my mind, was reflected in my mother, and I would rape. Say, for instance," he elaborates, "if I was sitting down with a lady and we're speaking. And she says something derogatory to me. I see more or less an image of my mother. I see my mother in her place. Mentally. It's a picture. When I get her alone I rape her. And when she

70

asks me why I done it, I tell her, 'Because you remind me of my mother, and I *hate* my mother—I don't want you like that.'

"The majority of my victims, I didn't get no trouble. I was rapin' them, right, and then actually sittin' down holdin' a conversation with them, drinking coffee or tea. And I'm sayin', 'I just raped this woman. What the hell is wrong with them?' I guess I was looking for something to happen, but nothing happened. It messed me up, because I'm looking for her to say, 'I'm gonna call the cops, I'm gonna kill you'—this and that and the other—and I didn't get it. It was a joke. They'd say, 'That's okay, that's okay.'"

Amos shakes his head in disbelief. "I don't think I really just chose people to rape them. It just came if the person was like my mother, I would rape 'em. It was a thing where I got to get this."

I ask Amos to backtrack a bit. "You said after you raped your sister you were sent to reform school, right?"

He nods.

"How old were you then?"

"Twelve or thirteen."

"What happened after your eighteen months in reform school?"

"When I went up there, I couldn't get into myself fully because I wasn't actually on the level to receive myself as I was. When I came out, I had various encounters with females."

He falls silent, then continues. "Like when a female plays with one's mind. You know, if you sit down and be truthful with a woman and then she—like, you know—tricks you up in some kind of manner. I think to release my anger towards her was through sexual gratification. I didn't actually want to bring harm to her or hurt her in the physical aspect, because I really didn't have that much control over me at that time. So I was out there, just running, and I really didn't have no concern for no one at that specific time in my life. So I was lonely, you know, with the family problems, et cetera."

"How many women did you actually rape?"

He shifts uncomfortably in his chair. His eyes survey the room as he makes a mental count. "I would say there was a good seven of them that I encountered with, and it came up to a thing whereas I would actually rape them—well, rape them in a sense."

"What do you mean by 'in a sense'?"

Amos scratches his chin. "In the sense whereas, um, say like for instance they were teasin', right, and then I just came out and asked for sex. And I was rejected by them, but the teasing continued. I would more or less grab them, force them down on the couch, whatever, and then do what I had to do as far as sex. And then I would get up and just leave. She'd see me on the street, or she'd see me the next day, and there'd be nothin' said." He shrugs his shoulders.

"As I got older, I got introduced to bars—swingin' bars, singles bars. And bein' in the New York area, I became very equipped with manipulatin' people with words and usin' people, whereas I had an older man more or less pimpin' to me. But at the same time I was pimpin' all the girls I encountered with, and the way I'd get them out on the streets was through sex. I would tie the girls maybe three or four days and leave 'em in the house. And when I come back they would do what I asked them to do. During this time I would have sex with them.

"At eighteen years old I got arrested for white slavery, or pimping. And I was dealing with youths. I had two thirteen and one fifteen. When I had these girls out on the street, out sellin' their bodies, I had their minds in my control. If I told them anything, they would do it.

"One day I had this encounter when I was dealin' in the bar. My first impression when I seen this young lady was that I didn't want to do nothin' 'cause I was in one of my sour states. And I just wanted to get high, drunk or whatever, to escape the reality. And she came over and probed and probed, sayin', 'What's a nice fellow like you doin' in a place like this?' I looked at her. I said, 'I'm not doin' nothin', mindin' my business,' whatever. She asked me if I would like to come to her apartment. Yeah, why not. And when I got there she came on saying, 'The only way I'll let you have my body is you got to rape me.'

"That messed me up, because all my life I've been taking women and then there's a person that's offerin'. But they want it in a way that I know I could produce. But I backed up from it because I feel messed up emotionally. It won't be rape. But in the event I did it. As soon as she turned around at the door and said I had to rape her, I looked at her and said, 'Whatever you want.' I just ripped off my clothes and had sex with her. Her husband came in, and this was a trip. Her husband says, 'I'm gonna kill you, you black mother,' and I'm sayin', 'Back up, it's not my fault.' He says, 'I'm takin' you to court, and I'm bringing your black ass to bear.' So he brought me to court.

"In the process of the trial all this had to come out—rape, this

and the other. And dealin' with the system we have today, I became very hostile in court. My lawyer told me to be cool, but I
flexed out. I said, 'Look, I know I'm gonna get burned for this.'
I'm not the type to be prejudiced—I want to establish that now—
but at that time I hated courts. I hated authority because what it did
to me as a child. From nine years old to twenty-seven bein' in and
out of prison—it's a trip. I told 'em, I said, 'I know I'm goin' to
jail.' If I didn't touch her, if I had been walkin' down the street and
something had occurred to this nature, I would have went to jail for
it if I had been in the area."

"You mean they would have arrested you because of your
prison record?"

Amos nods. "This is the way those people operate. So therefore, do what you have to do. 'I have nothing to say in my own
behalf,' I told my lawyer. 'I have no behalf in this.' Then I got sent
away," he concludes bitterly.

"Why did it turn you off when she said you should rape her?"
Sally asks.

He shrugs. "I guess when someone has hostility built up in
them, it makes it pressing, right? And if you play a game with
yourself and then the game's exposed to you, you back away from
it. This is how I felt. Like I would have raped her, like if it was a
thing where I was in one of my lustful states, something I looked at
and I gotta have it, and she says no, I'm gonna get it.

"But the vibes I got from her when she says, 'You have to
rape me,' it kicked up a nerve. I hunched my shoulders, and something just went through me. It's a feeling—I can't even explain it.
It was just like a cold shiver. Then I got hot. Then I did it anyway,
right? But in that one session, knowin' that she wanted to be raped,
I really didn't have no gratification out of doin' it."

"When did you rape again?"

He answers swiftly. "The second rape was with a school-
teacher."

"A schoolteacher?"

"She was every bit the image of my mother," he says harshly.
"'Amos, you gotta do this; Amos, you gotta do that'—I couldn't
stand her. I used to humiliate her. I used to come to school, I used
to hit her in the ass with paper clips because I hated her, man." His
face clouds with anger. "But she used to pass me every trip, but I
just couldn't stand her—you know, her ways, the way she would
carry herself, her conduct—and she had a very strange look. It

73

made me paranoid. I didn't like it. She would look at me, she would squinch her eyes"—he does an imitation of his old school-teacher—"like if to say, 'I'm waitin' for you to do something wrong.' It was like a testin' thing. This is when I was thirteen.

"The rape took place in school. Another fellow that I used to hang with, he was feelin' up a girl in class, and I was smackin' at him. And the teacher turned around and caught me in motion. She says, 'Get out of here.' She raised her voice at me, right? When she did that, I jumped up and I looked at her and said, 'I'm gonna kill you.' Just like that I went off on her. And in the process of me going off on her, she said, 'Amos, leave me alone.' And she was backin' off. I threw her down the stairs, and I told everyone to get out of the class. Behind the desk I threw her down. I ripped off her bra—everything—and as I was raping her I kept saying in her ear, 'I hate you, I hate you, you remind me of my mother.' I kept saying this constantly in her ear."

"What happened next?"

He takes a deep breath before replying. "After I had sexual intercourse with her, I got up, looked at her, and I was gonna hit her, but I didn't. And then I just walked out of the room. The cops came to my mother's house that afternoon and said, 'We have to take him.' They put me in a detention home. They said, 'Well, we can't send him upstate because he's too emotional at this time to actually deal with other people.'"

"When you were raping all those other women, how did you go about it?" I ask, changing the subject. "Did you stake them out, or what?"

"On occasions. Like I would look at people, and I might see a particular girl I want to have. And she might appear to me to have her nose up in the air—high-class, right? And I would squat on her."

"What do you mean by 'squat on her'?"

Amos grins at my confusion. "Squat meaning by waiting on her. This one particular case when I was young I seen this girl. She was fourteen. She had a body that was tremendous. She had a woman's body at age fourteen." Amos raises his hands to his chest and amplifies his remarks with a broad gesture. "I saw her comin' from school—I just happened to be around school that day—and I saw her and said I want her. But I wanted her to love me. I didn't want to rape. I really dug her. I was really into her," he says with apparent conviction.

74

"I was kinda shy with words to actually express myself to her, comin' from a man's point of view to a woman—my emotional feelings or whatever. I think that's because of the fact that my mother gave me a set pattern of rejection. In the event she rejected me when I approached her, said, 'Get lost, I don't want to bother with you.'

"I waited until the day of the prom. I didn't go to the dance or nothin', I just waited outside. When she came out I knocked her boyfriend out, threw her in the car. I had an assistant this trip. He's dead now. He got caught in the act in a bedroom and got killed. He had the car, and I threw her in the back seat. I gagged her, and we took off to the mountains. And we raped her, we sodomized her, and we did everything to her. She dug it."

Sally asks Amos if he wanted the girl to "dig it."

"No, I didn't want her to dig it," he says emphatically. "It's not like I was just goin' out to get a piece and say cool and back off. I was really hung up into this rape. I don't know why. I don't know what pushed me to that point." He falls into a pensive silence.

"Did you use any weapons or violence during the rape?" Sally asks.

"No, not to the point to bring physical harm," he replies. "I threatened them and would run a knife across their neck."

"What kind of feelings did you have when you did it?"

Amos takes time to think about the question. "Gratification, 'cause I actually thought it was my mother. I never wanted to have sex with my mother, I wanted to kill her. I really hate her to this day."

Our allotted time with Amos is at an end. We again wish him luck on his exam and pending release. He says he hopes he's been of assistance in our research and quietly leaves the room.

Kasim, age 23, was charged with rape in the first degree and sodomy in the first degree. He was sentenced to Green Haven Correctional Facility for twelve to twenty-five years. Kasim has refused parole and is seeking a retrial.

> *"Loose women. That's the type I'd rape.*
> *Night-goers. Women who hang out in bars. . . .*
> *I think women should take a better moral*
> *code upon themselves."*

Kasim enters the visiting room and greets us with a cheerful good-morning. A tall man with a small beard and a shy smile, he wears a knitted hat over his shaven skull. He engages us in some small talk about prison food, which he describes in highly unflattering terms. Kasim seems to be in a particularly buoyant mood; perhaps it's his jailhouse conversion to Islam that accounts for his sunny disposition.

"Let's start off with some of your background," I say.

"I lived in the ghetto. You can go from there about the type of life it was."

77

"How was your relationship with your father?"

"He died when I was eleven years old."

"What about your mother?"

Kasim nervously folds and unfolds his hands as he replies. "She was always warm, never changed," he says gently. "Always the same way. She would take nobody's side. If you're right, you're right. If you're wrong, you're wrong. She was a simple woman. She sent her children to school and told them to get good marks so she could show it off. She just wanted you to get what you needed to survive in this society. And that's what she gave us, all of us—six of us." He smiles broadly.

"Were you the oldest?"

"Next to the oldest. There were never no demands made on us. She always left it up to us."

"How was it growing up in your teens without a dad?"

He sighs. "It was rough. We were always looking for a father image. I never looked up to my older brother. He was hooked up on his things. He was doing things that wasn't very ideal to me. That killed the father image. I just forgot about it. I realized that one day I might have to be a father, so I created an image of my own."

"Can you think of anything in your younger days that may have led you to rape?"

"I had a very bad drinking life," Kasim says, shaking his head. "Blackouts. I don't even have no recollection that I raped this woman. If you read my psychiatric report or what my lawyer wrote, you can see that there's still some question in my mind whether I raped her or not. I'll say yes because of the evidence that came up about me during the trial."

"Tell us about it the best you can."

Kasim thoughtfully yanks at his beard. There is evidently something else on his mind. "When I was sixteen, seventeen, maybe eighteen, I had a woman that was a little older than me, maybe three or four years. She told me she was pregnant. I could spot a woman who was pregnant, being around my mother a lot, who taught me these different things. I told her I knew the child wasn't mine and if ever the child was born that I would take care of it. I kept my word to that effect. She was looking for me like somebody to dump a child on. She had no interest in it. That's what I didn't see." He smiles bitterly. "I thought it was all about sex. I didn't know you had to look at what type of character a woman had even before you get to sex—the mother she would make for your children. Sex is not even a question.

"When she found out that I knew and that I had no feelings toward her, she became very rebellious. So one night she takes the baby—four weeks old—out in the rain with no blanket on her. Just diapers. The baby catches pneumonia, and it dies. When that happened I rejected any woman—all women were the same," he concludes, glancing at Sally.

"What do you mean, you rejected women?" I ask.

"I blamed all women for being the same as her. If it was something I was doin' wrong, I don't think she should have taken it out on the kid."

"So you thought all women were like that?"

He simply nods.

"How did this affect your relationships with women?"

"Very bad," he says glumly. "I had a woman once tell me, 'Man, why don't you trust me?' I said, 'Is there any reason why I should trust you?' She became very rebellious and said all women are not alike. She said, 'I don't know what happened to you in your past life, but I can see by certain things you say to me that you try to hurt me.' She was right. I did try to hurt her."

"Do you hate women, or is it just that you don't trust them?" Sally asks.

"I don't know whether I can call it hate or not, but I spent most of my life trying to get even. There were women that I liked, but I never pushed the issue."

"But even the women you liked—was it in the back of your mind to hurt them, to get even?"

He nods.

"Can you describe the rape for us?"

"Like I told you, I don't remember too much about it. She was a neighborhood woman who claims to have known me. I have no recollection of her, of seeing her other than in the courtroom. And she said that I raped her." He pauses for a moment before continuing.

"Now, getting a woman without forcing her is a problem I never had. I never had any problems communicating with a woman." He falls silent, evidently reluctant to talk further about the rape.

"So you don't remember this woman at all?"

"Not too much."

"Were you drinking at the time?"

"Yeah, always. There was almost no time you could find when I wasn't high on some sort of barbiturate, wine, marijuana."

"There's a lot of dark spaces in your memory about a lot of things, is that right?"

"Yeah."

"Do you remember anything about how you met her and how the whole thing started?"

Kasim reflects on the question. "According to what the court says, she was coming out of the park near where I live and I stopped her. I asked her why she was in the park this late. She said I grabbed her by the arm and led her back into the park. She said I did a lot of weird things, that I made her take her clothes off. It was pretty cold out there—snow. And I just made her stand in the cold with her clothes off." He shakes his head in disbelief.

"What else did you do?"

"She said I began to talk about my hatred for women. And that's something I never did—not even to my mother, even though my mother wanted me to talk about *that* woman, the one that let the baby die. I objected. I didn't want to talk about it. But she said I said a lot of strange things."

"Well, how did you rape her?" I ask.

"She says I raped her, committed sodomy on her, and made her give me a blow job." He shakes his head again.

"Did you use a weapon?"

"No. No weapons involved. That's why I find it kind of hard. She said I had no weapons. I don't go nowhere without a weapon—especially in Bedford Stuyvesant. The officers said there was no weapon in my possession. They mentioned something about a toy gun. A gun is something I never carry. If it wasn't a knife, it was a machete that I'd carry."

"So you don't remember *anything* before, during, or after the rape?"

"No, not really."

"How were you arrested?"

"They arrested me on the scene of the crime. They said she had her clothes on. I don't know if I told her to put them on or what." His eyes survey the floor.

"They arrested you right in the park?"

"She said I walked her out of the park, where I met some of my friends. She said I waved a passing police car to confess my crimes."

"The police said you confessed?"

80

"The police said they remembered us coming out of the park. They said we were walking arm in arm. They said they thought it was a mistake and that we were together, so they kept on driving. After she reported the rape they remembered me." He falls silent again.

"I have doubts in my mind," Kasim adds without prompting. "I think it's something where I just mistreated her. If I were drinking, I just might do something like that. If I was sure I wouldn't have gone to trial, I would've just pleaded guilty to it."

"You mean you think you did it?"

"In a way. The way it came out, I might have done something. The one thing she said, I flagged a cop . . ."

I interrupt, trying to get past what the woman said to his own version of events. "She wasn't a complete stranger to you?"

"I'd seen her maybe once or twice. But to know her, talk to her, or even want to go out with her—no."

"How do you feel about the rape?"

"The rape, with the turmoil that she went through, it doesn't faze me."

"Why doesn't it faze you?"

Kasim shrugs. "I feel about her the same way I felt about the child. I just didn't care."

"What are your thoughts about rape?" Sally asks.

He ponders for a moment. "To take sex from a woman, I can't see me doing it—taking it like that if I was conscious and knew exactly what I was doing. Just the idea of knowing what I was doing would turn me off. Like anytime I did anything to a woman, it was quite some time before she actually knew I was doing it.

"I told a woman once, I asked her, 'Well, how would you feel if you were approached by a man and raped?' She looked at me kind of strange. I guess if she didn't know me, she'd probably call the cops. She asked, 'Why would you ask me something like that?' I said, 'Just for the information, you know. I wanted to know how it would feel if something was taken from you like that.' She said somebody who would do something like that, she would report it."

"Did you know what was going on during your trial?"

"Yeah, I knew what was going on."

"Did you think you were insane at the time?"

He shakes his head no. "I believed I did do it. I've been down here five and a half years. I know myself. I know things that I would do. I wouldn't rape anything—it would have to be a woman of a certain type."

81

THE RAPIST FILE

Both Sally and I are having trouble following Kasim. His recollections seem confused and contradictory, and it's hard to know what questions to ask.

"A few of the things makes me believe I did it," he continues. "The suffering part of it, the weird things she said I did to her. I believe I might just do something like that. I might just put her through those types of changes."

"You said you'd rape certain types of women. What types?" Sally asks.

"Loose women. That's the type I'd rape. Night-goers." His expression is sullen, and he almost spits the words.

"Do you think women ask to be raped?"

He purses his lips. "Most of them. A woman brought up in the proper environment, if she's raped it's just a freak accident."

"What do you mean by 'night-goers'?"

"Women who hang out in bars."

"Can you say more about that?"

"It could be a single woman or even be women who are with their husbands. If you take a woman into an environment where she doesn't belong and expect that courtship or marriage to last, you have very little knowledge about relationships. Because there's always somebody who wants your woman or some woman that wants your man. So there's no real relationship to take a woman into that kind of environment and have your woman meet you in that type of place. So evidently they don't care."

"It sure sounds like if you were on the streets again all these women would be potential rape victims for you."

He shrugs. "I don't think anything would change my feelings towards them."

"You mean you still hate women because of that baby thing?"

"I do, I hate them. I do," he says, clenching his fists. "It's for that kind of clientele. I've met beautiful women—and when I'm speaking of a woman, I'm not speaking of pigmentation, I'm talking about something for that woman that a man fails to see. I've never had that kind of woman, but I know she exists—where you don't have to wonder what type of woman she is, what type of family circle she will create. I don't feel ashamed about the things I've done to women. I hurt a lot of them, but they deserved it."

I decide to try a different kind of question. "When you wrote us that we could interview you, you said that you'd adopted a religion."

"I'm a Muslim," he says proudly.

82

"If that's the case, why do you view women with such intense hatred? Is that what your religion teaches you?"

He smiles. "I understand what you're saying, but you can't take a person out of an environment and expect them to live accordingly to what I just described. They have to take themselves, or something has to be done to make them see that the way they are is not the type of life they should lead. They're out there, and whatever happens to them is exactly what they're asking."

"So in order to get women to conform with the lifestyle you would like to see them live, you would rape them? You felt they deserved to be raped?"

"I'm not saying they deserve to be raped. I wouldn't want any woman to be raped in the very sense of the word rape. I wouldn't want any woman—regardless of how I feel about her—to go through that ordeal. But if a woman puts herself in that type of position and does nothing to change it, or gets raped in a certain environment and goes back to that same environment, what does that tell you? That it's her, it's her and not the rapist that's raping her. She's putting herself in the position to be raped."

"Hanging out in bars doesn't make a woman a bad person," Sally protests. "Are you saying that any woman who has a drink at a bar is asking to get raped?"

Again he shrugs. "I think women should take a better moral code upon themselves. You can tell the environment of a person by their personality—that moral code I spoke of previously—even if they try to hide it. And I've had women who have tried to hide it to try and please me. A man has a moral code just the way a woman has a moral code. He has certain things that he's just not going to do. There's certain environments you're not going to go into or adhere to. The same with women. You have a woman in those types of environments, like bars, and they'll lie to themselves just to satisfy the people who are in there. That's how prostitutes are made.

"Ninety-nine percent of your prostitutes come from your best of homes. But after they reach a certain point as far as education is concerned, they found out that they weren't acceptable. So they went into different environments—they took jobs here, they took jobs there. I know a specific prostitute who was a neurologist, a doctor. When she found she couldn't be accepted in that type of environment—she was married to a nice doctor and found something phony about that—she went seeking something else."

83

Again I don't quite know what to make of his convoluted reasoning. I decide to change the subject. "Would you want to meet the woman you raped?"

"No. Right now, knowing what I've done to women—regardless of their moral code—I'm beginning to see in very small instances that all women are not all alike. I wouldn't want to do anything or say anything psychologically that they'd be able to pick up which would hurt them."

"What would you say if the woman you raped walked into the room this instant?" Sally asks.

"I don't know. It's something . . . I couldn't say. Like if I was just talking to her, I would find it difficult to talk to her. Just like I find it difficult to answer most of your questions."

"What are your masturbation fantasies like?"

Kasim answers hesitantly. "Masturbation with me is very difficult because I find it all so hard to fantasize on something if I don't have it. As far as those pornography books go, they're not too much help. If it's not the real thing it doesn't affect me. It's very hard for me to masturbate. So I don't really think about masturbating."

"Have you had sex with other inmates?"

"I couldn't screw guys. I couldn't get into it on the street, so I'm not gonna do it here."

"Have you been raped while in prison?"

"I don't put myself in that environment in here with all the guys drinking wine, getting in debt through cards. I stay mostly to myself. I don't indulge and everything." Kasim seems anxious to end the interview.

"Do you have anything to add?"

"You should concentrate on what brings about rape. Rape is a sexual and violent act. If you were sexually oriented in this society and then turned to something violent—this is where you get your rapist from. He's constantly being fed. That's why I don't go to a lot of them movies. One week they may show nothing but X-rated films—nothing but sex, people in bed. I don't call that sex. That's a complete distortion. But the way the minds of people are working today, that's what's being accepted as sex—that ejaculation, that climax.

"Then the next week they go to a Superfly film full of murder and a little more sex. The next scene is more murder. That's an orientation. A person who goes out on the streets, and he sees

Superfly, and the reality is happening in the neighborhood—then you got yourself a rapist," Kasim concludes. "Where else is he going to turn? He grew up in that environment. He does the same thing as in the movies."

Part II

LOUISIANA STATE PENITENTIARY

The JFK airport lounge is bustling with travelers trying to steel jittery nerves with booze and cigarettes. A harried bartender asks us what ours is, and we order a couple of beers. He fills our glasses with the frothy stuff, and it seems to wipe away the taste of prison grime that I've had in my mouth since we left Green Haven just a couple of hours ago.

Two women seated at an adjoining table are engaged in an animated conversation. One of them is complaining that the refrigerator she recently purchased doesn't work properly. Her companion nods sympathetically. Sally and I exchange amused glances. It's a relief to be back in the world of everyday problems and mundane concerns. Just listening to the two women helps ease the shock both of us feel after spending two days inside the walls of Green Haven. I order a couple more beers. They go down well.

I check my watch, and it's almost time for us to board our plane for the first leg of our journey to Louisiana State Penitentiary, also known as the "Alcatraz of the South." Tomorrow it begins all over again. Two more days of intensive interviewing, more questions to ask, more brutal stories to listen to, and—if we're lucky— some pertinent answers.

The early-morning drive to the prison takes us deep into the damp belly of bayou country. It is a swampy wonderland of tropical colors and strange, overgrown vegetation. The winding highway seems to be our only real link to civilization. At lengthy intervals along the road there are lonely reminders that the area isn't entirely devoid of human habitation. We pass a small post office, a diner, and a lumber mill.

Despite the heat, a chill snakes down my spine. This lush desolation is a perfect setting for the eighteen-hundred-acre prison farm located somewhere nearby. I doubt whether anyone has ever successfully escaped from Louisiana State Penitentiary: if the guards don't get you, the gators and water moccasins will.

Sally says something to me, and I nearly jump out of my skin, causing the car to veer slightly.

"Nervous?" she asks.

"Aren't you?"

89

THE RAPIST FILE

Louisiana State Penitentiary springs up where the road ends. It is a stagnant-green fortress with a manned tower at the front gate. Beyond the gate are hundreds of acres of prison farmland that keep the prisoners busy. The penitentiary is located in Angola, a town whose name derives from a Latin term meaning "place of anguish." The long history of the penal institution has done little to diminish that reputation. It is reported that in 1951, thirty-seven inmates severed their left heel tendons with razor blades to protest their treatment. And in slave times, the penitentiary land was worked as a giant sugar plantation.

Our car is halted at the prison gate, where a blue-uniformed guard asks us to identify ourselves. With his sun-scorched face and cowboy hat, he looks like something straight out of a chain-gang movie. His hand dangles loosely over the butt of his revolver.

After checking his master visitors' list, he drawls, "You got any guns, alcohol, or dangerous drugs in the car?"

"We have a couple of cans of beer in the back seat," I admit sheepishly. He makes us feel like we've been on a binge the night before.

The guard politely asks us to remove the cans and places them in a small locker. His search of the car also turns up some cigarette ashes, which he sniffs suspiciously. Satisfied that they are just that—cigarette ashes and not marijuana—he waves us through.

I ask him where the rapists are being held.

"Go straight down the road into the second building on the left. They'll have the people y'all want to see waitin' for you."

We start down the paved road that leads past the administrative building, a ranch-style structure in front of which two inmates are carefully tending some shrubbery. A bit farther down the road is the infirmary, and just up ahead the A building—our destination.

Inside, we are ushered to a small holding area where inmates wait for their release papers or for visitors. Several men are seated on wooden benches. A name is called, and a sandy-haired inmate approaches the gate that separates the area from the outside. Carefully clutching a battered shoebox, he takes his release papers and leaves under escort, without once turning back.

The correctional officer on duty double-checks his list of daily visitors and, without asking for any further identification, opens the gate for us. We are led into an interview room just a trifle larger than the one at Green Haven. It's stifling hot and windowless.

"They're all out there waiting for you," he tells us, indicating the holding area. "Which one do you want to see first?"

Sally and I quickly review our list of names. "Willy will be okay," I tell the guard.

He nods and leaves to bring in the prisoner.

Willy, age 24, was sentenced to life imprisonment for aggravated rape. He has served seven years at Louisiana State Penitentiary and is not eligible for parole.

"I've been caught for rape before in Missouri, but the law is different up there than it is down here. See, up there if you rape a white woman, first thing a security officer might say he understands or that's your woman, because there ain't no racist thing up there. Black live with white."

We have barely had time to set up our recording equipment when Willy enters the room. He is wearing a white sweater with "Little T" crayoned on the sleeves. His hair is in pigtails, his head is wrapped in a red bandanna, and he sports a single golden earring.

Sally leads off the interview with the usual question about Willy's background. He responds very politely, almost obsequiously, in a thick Louisiana drawl.

93

"I was born in Mississippi, raised in Baton Rouge, Louisiana. I've been to the home a lot of times on different charges—burglary, auto theft, cuttin' my sister one time."

"How was your relationship with your parents?"

He shrugs indifferently. "They was close to me. I wasn't close to them. They cared a lot about me, but I couldn't get things right myself. My mother treated me like a god, but I didn't accept it, though. I feel like I had a mental problem at that time. I did things sometimes for spite, just like this charge I'm on now. It came mostly out of spite too. My dad treated me like a god too, but it was just something where I couldn't cross that line with them. It's always been like that up to now. They come to see me every other week. But if they don't come to see me, I don't worry about it."

"How do they feel about what you've done?"

"I know they feel bad. They'll probably ask me why I did it, what reason. I could never give them no reason because it was just one of them things that night—spur of the moment there. It just happened." Without further prompting, Willy launches into an account of the incident. He seems eager to talk about it.

"It was three of us, we was goin' down the streets. This woman, her and her husband was settin' on the porch. We passed 'em the first time. By me bein' black in that part of the neighborhood at that time of night, they just made some smart remarks. So we kept goin' and doubled back. They was still settin' on the porch."

"How old were you at the time?"

"Sixteen."

"Where did this take place?"

"In Baton Rouge. So I pulled my pistol out, and I ran up to the porch and told 'em to hold it—don't move. So the man, he throwed me his wallet. He felt like I was comin' after the money. She had her purse sittin' there, so she throwed her purse too. So I told them no, they should come off the porch. So when they came out in the yard, I locked her husband in the trunk and put the wife inside of the car." He pauses.

"How old was she?"

"About twenty-one. So all of us got in the car. We drove around for awhile. I was plannin' on killin' her myself. The raping part of it came up, and she decided she'd do anything we want—just don't kill her." He flashes us a smile and continues his narrative. "So we made a big joke out of the thing. We hollered through the back seat to the trunk to her husband. We asked him if it was

94

all right makin' a big joke out of it. We raped her about three times. After we raped her, we drove around with them awhile, still deciding should we kill 'em.

"Somehow she convinced us that by killin' her we'd get it. We didn't kill 'em. We cut 'em loose. About ten minutes later the police had surrounded us. Took us downtown. I told 'em we didn't do it. So they put us in the lineup, took pubic hair samples. She picked me out for sure, 'cause she remembered the pistol I had. They got me dead right on this here." He grins.

"What did the husband say all this time?" I ask.

"He just said one thing—we wasn't going to get away with it. We didn't pay no attention to him. If he gave us any trouble beside what he did, he wouldn't have seen the trial."

"What was the woman's reaction?" Sally asks.

Willy smiles nastily. "She was cryin'. She was askin' us don't do it. If I'm not mistaken she claimed she was pregnant. She forced that upon herself."

"What do you mean, she brought it on herself?"

"I kind of feel like this here—if she wouldn't have made the remarks, just by her appearance at that time this would have happened anyway."

"I don't understand," Sally says. "What about her appearance?"

"She had on some blue jeans, it would take axle grease to put 'em on or take 'em off," Willy explains. "Titties way out." He grins again and gestures suggestively. "Then she was half-dressed anyway. It just seemed like she was just messing with our minds." He gives Sally a searching glance.

"She was lookin' for some trouble. We weren't really lookin' for nobody to rape, but if there was another woman half-dressed like that, she'da probably got the same thing. If a woman don't want to be messed with out there . . . it's just like if you have twenty-five dollars and you go downtown and you see a dress cost fifty—you gonna get it, right? She showed us something we wanted. We know we couldn't get it unless if we take it. That's what we did. We took it."

"How did you feel about taking something like that?" I ask.

He shrugs. "At the time it bother me. Since I've been up here, I've seen so much stuff bein' took. . . . Just like when I first came up here, they asked me what am I charged with. 'I'm charged with rape,' I told them. They said, 'White woman? Well, we got a place for you. Put you where you'll be raped at.' They tried. I was for-

95

tunate I had two brothers up here. Security was pushin' the issue. That was their sole intention for it to happen—for me to be raped. If it was a black woman it probably would have been the same thing. They just don't like that there. You can kill somebody, that's cool. Steal somethin', they say you're surviving. But takin' a woman's body, black or white, they can't see it. They'd rather get you messed over too."

Willy continues to talk randomly about prison conditions. I'm about to ask a question when he offers a piece of unsolicited information. It seems that his career as a rapist was not terminated by his incarceration in Louisiana State Penitentiary. During the years he has been locked up here, he has continued to rape with the same viciousness he displayed on the outside—only now his victims are fellow inmates.

"You mean you've been raping guys in here?" I ask without concealing my surprise.

He grins and nods his head. "If I see something up here I want, I rape it up here," he says. "It's their appearance, the way they carry on. They might go put on some tight pants, tie their head up. They're showing me that they got more female than anything. If I ask 'em for it and they don't give it to me, then there's only one thing left to do—and that's take it."

"How many times have you raped in here?"

"I couldn't count it. It ain't no everyday thing, it ain't no once-a-year thing. I try to rape somebody three times a week."

"Three times a week?"

He nods.

"Does raping these guys affect your manhood?" I ask.

"Well, it's like this," Willy explains. "When I do something like that there, it don't tear me down. It's making me feel bigger, stronger." He puffs up his chest. "When I do something like that, and if I attempt to rape one and I don't rape one, then that tears me down then. I look at it the other way around. If he wouldn't have been so scared, he probably could have raped me."

"Have any of the inmates you raped reported it?"

The expression on Willy's face bluntly informs me that he finds the question naive. "They too scared to report it," he says. "And the only way security might take action is if an inmate is raped and he threatens to tell his peoples about it. Then they take you and lock you up. But really nothing else happens to you."

"Tell us more about the inmates you've raped," Sally says.

"Yez, ma'am." He pauses. "You go mess with them, some of 'em might put up a little struggle. Some of 'em might try to talk their way out of it. But somebody like me, I don't want to hear that talk. I go in for one thing, and I ain't gonna accept any other thing. If I go at their body, that's what I want—their body. If they don't give me their body, I might kill 'em. I ain't never killed none up here yet. But then again, I ain't missed too many of them.

"Like I say, I got a weak mind. They lead me on. They do something to turn me on, that's the first thing that comes to my mind. Whereas a woman might wear a short dress out there, she's gonna attract the male eyes. The inmates up here, they tie their head up with a colored bandanna, put on some tight pants—that signifies. I can look at one of the inmates and think about some girl I raped out there on the street. That's the way I do it, anyway."

"Do you ever think about the woman in the car?"

"I think about it at times. I don't think I shouldn't have done it. I think of how good it was. I don't let it worry me about should I did it or not. I'll never be sorry for nothing I do. I did it, and I'm serving life. But I'm proud to say one thing—I ain't serving life like some inmates who are serving life for nothing. See, I took that. See, I can go to bed and sleep."

"How many other rapes have you committed?"

"I lived in Kansas City and Chicago. I can't count them, there were so many," he boasts.

"You can't count them?"

Willy shrugs. "I've been caught for rape before in Missouri, but the law is different up there than it is down here. See, up there if you rape a white woman, first thing a security officer might say he understands or that's your woman, because there ain't no racist thing up there. Black live with white. They kept me locked up for about six months, and they cut me loose in my parents' custody. I was twelve then. I was nine when I started."

"You were nine years old when you began raping?" Sally asks.

He nods, clearly amused by her incredulity.

"Could you tell me about that first time?" Sally asks.

"Yez, ma'am. See, it really started with a fight a brother and a sister had, and there was about thirteen of us. And the girl's brother, he got killed. We thought we had beat him up—he was laying on the ground. I couldn't say how the sex thing came about on her. All I know we was just at it. We didn't want to cut her loose. And like the longer we held her, the gooder it got. So we

97

continued holding her then."

I ask him if he always raped while in the company of his friends.

"It don't matter if I'm with a bunch of guys and a woman shows me something I want. I'm going at it whether they come with me or not. There ain't no special color. If they show me something, they can be green. I'm gonna get it."

"At what age did most of the rapes you committed take place?"

"About fourteen. I raped 'em everywhere. See, my aunt lived in Chicago, my mother lived in Louisiana, my grandmother stayed in Missouri. When I'd get in trouble in one state, I'd go to another to beat the charge. All through Mississippi—I raped women goin' through Mississippi. At the bus stop. I raped 'em in Louisiana, Chicago, and I raped in Missouri." He sounds extremely proud of himself. "Hell, I was like a UFO. You could see me in Kansas City today and Chicago tomorrow. If I caught one along the way in Saint Louis, she was raped."

"How did you go about doing it?"

He leans forward in his seat and motions with his hands as he speaks. "See, if I walk out that door now and a woman passin' by there half-dressed—she's caught, she's trapped. Only way she can get away, she go up in some business place where some more people's at. And if I figure she ain't gonna be there too long, I will wait on her. Other than that, if she don't go into some business place, she half-dressed, *I got her*. Some of 'em be wearing no bra, some of 'em be wearing hip-huggers that sets down on their hips—all their backsides be out like they're telling you to come and get it.

"I don't never get caught without a pistol, 'cause there are policewomen out there now. I may be stupid on one matter, but I ain't stupid in all. All that screamin' and hollerin', that would do nothin' but get her shot. I'd have to. I ain't never shot none of 'em, but I pistol-whipped a lot of 'em."

He gives Sally a ferocious glance before continuing. "They understand, they get the message then. They have to make me do violence. See, I'm gonna rape them either way they go—whether they holler or not. They only make it harder for theirself when they holler, 'cause you know I don't want nobody to hear. So I'm gonna do the best thing I can to shut her up. If beatin' her up is gonna shut her up, well, then I'll do it. If that ain't gonna stop her, well, then I don't care if I shoot her."

"Would anything stop you or turn you off?" I ask.

98

He smiles meanly. "Yeah, kill me or the police come. Other than that, there's nothing she can do."

"What if she was really in pain?" Sally asks.

Willy glares at her. "I don't feel no pain. How do I know she's bein' in pain? I wouldn't stop at that—like that woman who said she was pregnant. But that go in one ear and out the other with me."

I'm still a bit amazed that Willy began to rape when he was nine—something I didn't think was possible—so I question him again on that point. "How many girls did you rape at age nine?"

He laughs. "Lots of 'em. Little girls, neighborhood girls about my age."

"What made you become a rapist?"

He thinks for a few seconds. "After I got up here, the only thing that I could see that would make me do it, that they were half-dressed. If a woman passes me by half-dressed—she raped. Just like in the shower here. If I go in there and see somebody look good, something's gonna happen."

"What's the oldest woman you ever raped?"

"Well, there was this woman, she was seventy-eight years old, in Baker, Louisiana. I was fifteen at the time. She tricked us—sent us to the store. When we come back, she wouldn't even let us in the home. She didn't give us what she promised us. She promised us to pay for goin' to the store. Besides killin' or beatin' up, that's the next best thing I know—to rape. I believed that that's what she wanted. The only resistance she put up was keepin' the door closed. When we got in the house it seemed that she was for us. Like she volunteered to do all this on her own. I didn't have to beat her up. It seemed like she wanted it just as bad as we wanted it."

Our time with Willy is almost at an end. I thank him for his cooperation, but he just sits there.

"You can go now," I say.

"Yez, sir," he replies, and reluctantly leaves the room.

99

Ben, age 30, was charged with forcible rape. He has served three years of a twenty-year sentence at Louisiana State Penitentiary and is seeking parole under special circumstances.

"And if thy right eye offend thee, pluck it out and cast it from thee: for it is profitable for thee that one of thy members should perish, and not that thy whole body should be cast into hell . . ."
Matthew 5:29

A thin, nervous inmate enters the visiting room and gives us a barely audible hello, as if he's afraid he's interrupting something. Ben takes a seat and immediately lights the first of several cigarettes. He's very fair-haired, with a trace of golden mustache. Despite the summer heat, he's wearing a blue woolen cap that matches the color of his eyes. He has a shy, reserved manner, and he begins fidgeting in his chair even before the interview gets underway.

101

Sally leads off the questioning, asking him to tell us something about his childhood.

He says that as a boy he never got along with his father, who used to whip him.

"How did your mother react when he did that?"

Ben smiles anxiously and plays with a matchbook that's lying on the table. "My mother was a hothead. I never heard my father cuss, but my mother cussed a whole lot," he says in a thick Southern accent. "And she more or less took care of my sister when it came to whipping. I remember a few times when she got us both, throwed things at us or throwed us out the back door." He frowns at the memory.

"But I think it was a sad relationship. I did a lot of thinkin' these past few years, and I think they tried to raise me the best way they knew how, even though it wasn't up to my comparison. I would have liked to been raised with a little more understandin' from my parents' part, and I wish I had a little more understandin' towards them.

"But my father, he never taught me anything, so what I learned I learned on my own, and I didn't learn anything. I didn't know what to learn or who to learn it from. And the reason why I just moved into the Marine Corps was for the simple reason to just get away from home, 'cause I wasn't gettin' along there." He takes a deep drag on his cigarette. There is a plaintive quality to everything he says.

"I never had any attention at home. I guess that's why I just started runnin'. I found out now that I was runnin' more from myself than anybody else. One thing led to another, and I wind up here."

Sally turns to the question of his first rape. Ben begins to tear the book of matches apart as he talks about it.

"Well, I was workin' for this cab company. I was married, but me and my wife was separated. I was goin' with this girl that I had met at this insurance company where I had to buy some high-risk insurance. Me and her was datin', goin' out or whatever. The whole time I was drivin' a cab, I was drinkin'. I didn't care about nothing—not even myself. While she was at this dinner party, I had borrowed her car and just went drivin' and gettin' drunk.

"So this woman happened to be in one of them bars that I stopped in. I was in there shootin' pool, and I bought her a couple of beers. I knew then what I was goin' to do. So when she started

102

to leave, I asked her if she wanted a ride home. She said okay, and when we got on the interstate, that's when I pulled a gun on her, took her out to the woods and did my thing."

"What was your 'thing'?" Sally asks.

He looks uncomfortable. "I made her have oral sex with me, and after that we made love." He pauses. "I tell you, that whole incident really scared me, because I wasn't gonna hurt her at all, I was just gonna put the scare of her life in her.

"So I had the twenty-two pistol I had been carrying with me for protection. So while we were having oral sex, she grabbed my pants and took off running—I had the car keys in my pants. Well, I chased her down and caught her, and I pulled her down to the ground and slapped her across the face. Not real hard, just enough to scare her. And then I went through the routine of just trying to scare her to make her behave herself so I wouldn't have to hurt her." Ben absently places his hand on his heart. "Because, lord, I didn't want to hurt her."

"So the gun was in the car. I had already unloaded it for her. So I took her by the arm and took her back to the car. And I told her, 'You're gonna behave, one way or the other.' And I got the gun from the car and put all the shells in it but one."

He shakes his head disapprovingly. "I stood there for a little while, and I was rotatin' that cylinder 'cause I left one chamber empty. So the next chamber up would be an empty chamber. That's why I tried settin' it that way. So I took her back up the road a little bit to where we was at first, and I started teasin' her with that gun while she was giving me oral sex. I had it in my hand just rubbin' her head with it. So I cocked it, and it was still pointin' at her head. I was gonna fire it on the blank empty chamber. So when I pulled it away from her head, the gun went off. It scared the livin' daylights out of me."

"When you had the gun at her head, did it make you hotter— did you like that feeling?" Sally asks.

Ben thinks for awhile before answering. "It wasn't so much the gun as it was her givin' me the blow job. It's just a dominant feeling, I guess. I enjoyed what I was doin', but it was wrong. I admit that.

"After it was all over with, I took her out to my boss man's house, and we stopped on the way, and I bought her a beer and a package of cigarettes. And I actually told him what I done—him and his wife. We left there, and I told her, I said, 'Look, I know

103

you're gonna get me in trouble, but I wish you wouldn't.' She was three months pregnant at the time.

"What really helped me out was that when I took her home she didn't call the police. She called these friends of hers and told her friends I was over there drunk, with a gun. And while they was on their way over they got stopped for speedin'. And that gave me a chance to get a cab and go home. They arrested me, and I got two years out of that one."

"You said you knew you were going to rape her?"

He nods.

"What was going on in your mind when you decided that?"

Ben ponders momentarily. "When I seen her I didn't really want no sex, because I was goin' with this other girl at the time. But when I saw her I knew I was goin' to do it. I don't know what it was, I just knew it. It's something like preparin' yourself to come down here. Somebody tells you you're comin' down here—well, it's a shock. But then, after you think about it awhile, you know you can handle it. I knew enough about her that I could do what I could do without hurting her."

"Did you feel any remorse immediately afterwards?"

"I didn't regret what I did," he says quietly. "I'm sorry that it happened, but I've got no regrets it did happen. But I've learned a lot down here, and what I did was because of what happened to me in my past. I just wasn't able to mature enough to evaluate things. And now I can look at things and know where my faults are and go from there.

"But I don't blame my family as much as I do myself. Everybody plays a part. Now, if my father and mother would have been better to me than what they did, and tried to teach me at an early age the things about life, I think things would have been different. But they let me go wild—plus the whippings. It gave me such an inferiority complex. I didn't have any friends at school. Even goin' to school, I ran from people. I resented people because of the way I was treated at home. I resented them through my parents. I've learned this.

"Take, for instance, the times I wet my bed. I'd wake up in the mornin', and my bed would be all wet, and I'm not able to take a bath before I go to school. And all the kids around me can smell me. And they'd make fun of me, and it just adds to the pain all the way through life. So I guess this was just a get-back for what someone had done to me. That's the only thing I can figure."

I ask Ben why he chose women rather than men to "get back at."

"That's a good question," he says, smiling and tapping the table. "Another intelligent human being I don't think would have stuck a gun to her head and pulled the trigger. Even though I've been hurt, I wouldn't deliberately try to hurt anybody. Even though I raped these two girls, I didn't hurt 'em in any way except just to embarrass them a little or hurt their pride. I don't think I could ever kill anybody, because I'm afraid of people. I think when I get out of here I'm just gonna live by myself. In twenty years I'll have enough money in my account to live by myself for the rest of my life," Ben concludes, glancing at us forlornly.

"I forgot one other little detail," he says, and begins tapping on the tabletop again. "When I was growin' up at home, at one time—they call it incest now—I thought that's what I was doin' with my sister. We would play little mature games. I would go to bed with her, and I'd even jack off between her legs. But I never entered her in any way, and I thought this was screwy. And we went on like this ever since I was about twelve until I was fifteen.

"When she started menstruating, she put it in." He scratches his head. "I think that had a lot to do with it too. We never got caught by my parents. There was one incident, after I came back from Colorado from doing time up there, that my sister let me play with her. But she said that after that there would be no more or she'd tell her boyfriend, and then all hell would break loose. Well, I got drunk one night and winded up telling him anyway. And he told my father—phew! I thought he was going to kill me." Ben actually shudders at the memory. "I never thought it was wrong until my father actually said something about it. But I was raised around a bunch of girls anyway—both next-door neighbors were girls, my sister was a girl, all my cousins were girls. But I never did associate with them all that much.

"All my life I've been just by myself. I don't know what I would have done if I had gone up to one and asked her for a date and one of 'em would have accepted. I think I would have fell dead right there. Even when I got in a fight I wouldn't fight back—just fear, total fear . . ."

"Tell us more about that first girl in the car. What did you do to her?" I ask.

He shifts in his chair. "Because I was pretty drunk, what I can remember was as we turned off the exit on the interstate, I had that gun on my hip in front of my shirt. I pulled it out and I cocked it and I pointed it at her. I said, 'You know what this is for?' She was so scared of that gun. 'Course, I knew that was going to happen already because, I mean, her actions—I knew that was going to be. And she said, 'Look, just put that thing away. Don't point it at me, don't cock it. I'll do anything you want.' So that suits me, you know, so I took the gun and unloaded it and laid it between the seat. I made her put her hand between my legs and unbutton a couple of buttons on her bra.

"I didn't really know where to go. I was just searching for a place. But I knew that in the general direction we was going there'd be a lot of woods. I looked in the back seat 'cause I thought that's where I wanted to do it at, but it was a small compact car, and I didn't want to get all cramped up. So we walked up the hill. I asked her if she'd ever given oral sex before. She said yeah. I guess that's what I wanted in the first place, because I wanted to make her swallow my come. I don't know, I guess I got too excited or whatever, and things weren't goin' right. We just had sex. She even acted like she enjoyed it.

"I had her hands in my hands, and her hands were above her head. I kept them up there. She asked me could she put her hands down. I said, 'Yeah, why don't you put them around me?' This is while we're having sex, and so about five minutes later she actually acted like she enjoyed it. But she didn't. I haven't been with very many girls, but I could tell she wasn't enjoyin' it. She was fakin' it all around." Ben suddenly falls silent. He is tearing at the matchbook again.

Sally asks whether he would have been turned off if the woman had struggled violently.

He laughs nervously. "I think it would have scared me enough so that I would have stopped."

"Tell us about the second rape."

"Well, this was a couple of years after. I spent from January to March on learning how to drive a truck while I was on parole. I even got a truck of my own to drive during this time. So in April I got a truck of my own, and I was on my first trip. My boss, he sent me to Clarksdale, Mississippi. He says, 'When you leave Clarksdale, come back through Monroe and see your daddy.' I says, 'No, I can't do that.' I says, 'I know if I go up there by myself with all this responsibility and this big truck, something's gonna happen.' He says, 'No, man, go see your daddy.'

106

"I kept arguing with him 'cause I didn't want to come through Monroe 'cause I'm gonna get into trouble. Believe it or not I really argued. So he had to give me a little extra money, because I told him there was this girl up there workin' at this truck stop. I said I could have a little fun up there before I went to Monroe. When I got there, she had already been arrested for prostitution, so that didn't work out.

"So anyway, I come to Monroe, and instead of going to my daddy's house, I parked the truck in the truck stop, dropped the trailer, and went to the nearest bar I could find. Well, not the nearest one, but the one I usually hang out with there. I was just showin' off because here I am with this big truck and makin' a good livin'. I wanted everybody to see my truck. So anyway, there was this old lady there that I called Godmother 'cause she don't drink. She just goes in there, drinks Cokes, and dances with the band. There was this heavyset girl sitting next to her, and I wound up taking her for a ride in my truck."

He shakes his head. "When I took her out to my truck, I was parked out there on the interstate right next to the bar. And when I backed up, I backed right up into this guy's car. I was drunk. I don't even know how I drove that truck. So I took her for a ride around the block, and I come back 'cause I had to call the police and have an insurance investigation. And while they took me to the police station, she went home. She left her phone number to give me.

"When I went over there to her house, I just got to thinkin'— the heck with it, I'm gonna get me some. So that's what I did. I went over there and parked the truck by the interstate and walked down to her house. Well, she met me at the door in this bikini, and that's all it took. There again, that feelin' come over me. I knew I was goin' to do it. I don't know why, but I just did. But this time I was scared because I hadn't prepared myself for it.

"So we went inside, and I didn't have no kind of weapon or anything, so I pretended to go to the bathroom and I went to the kitchen. I was gonna get a knife, and I couldn't find no knife." He laughs nervously. "So there's this meat fork in a drain ditch. So I picked it up and stuck it under my belt and went back into the room. We smoked a couple of joints. She gets this phone call, and I thought this would probably ruin it right then. She was fixin' to go out.

"So I walked over to her, more or less of a half-walk, half-

107

run, and I grabbed her by the hair. And she turned around, and I had that meat fork out. She started complaining. She said, 'Why are you doing all this?' I managed to throw her down on the bed, which was just a few steps." Ben makes a shoving motion with his hands.

"She grabbed my hand where the meat fork was, and I just started easing it down. It happened to puncture her neck, and that's what got me convicted—'cause it hit her neck. But I didn't mean to hit her in the neck. She kept asking me what I wanted, what I was going to do and all this. I didn't say nothin'. Then she started to scream. So I laid the meat fork down and grabbed her with my hand. There's a karate hold that you can put on a person, and if it's put just right she can't scream or nothin'." Ben demonstrates. "If she tries to bite you, it's more pressure on her than it is on your fingers.

"So she didn't scream anymore, so I kept thinkin' 'bout that dude comin' over. So I said, 'Look, we gonna walk. You take it real easy and you won't get hurt.' So we walked out of the bedroom into the bathroom. I thought about lettin' her put on some clothes, but she didn't have nothin' there that would slip over her head. So I said, 'We'll just walk over to the truck like this.' She's in her bikini. So as we started out the door, I looked down the street to see if anybody was comin', and this police car was comin' down the street. So I just eased back into the door."

Ben pauses to take a pull on his cigarette. "He saw me, but I don't know why he didn't stop or whatever. I bet he knew what was going on. If he didn't he should have, 'cause he seen the whole incident. 'Cause I had my hand in her mouth like that"—he demonstrates again—"and the meat fork in my hand.

"So I seen him and backed off in the door until he passed. And when he left we walked out to the truck. I told her to get in the sleeper and lay down on her stomach. When we got into the truck I laid the fork between the two seats. I told her to put her hands behind her back. I was gonna tie her up, gag her, and get away from there. And I was gonna go to the truck stop and pick up the trailer and drive off. So I started to tie her, and she said, 'What do you want to do, fuck?' And I said, 'Well, I guess so.' Just like that—'I guess so.' So we started makin' sex. She wouldn't let me kiss her, and I know why now. Because I had a partial plate in my mouth. All the teeth were missin' out of it. I guess she thought I had bad teeth or something. I took off her bikini, and we had sex.

LOUISIANA STATE PENITENTIARY

But this girl, regardless of what happened, she enjoyed it. She didn't act like it much, but she did."

Sally asks Ben what makes him believe that. He laughs, then becomes serious again.

"Well, when you go have sex with a girl and she's any kind of turned on, it won't be dry in the vagina. It will be sort of wet and slooshy. 'Cause I know the times I made love to my wife, when she didn't enjoy it, it would be dry and hard goin' in. But this girl was different. 'Cause I think she enjoyed it as much as I did."

"Do you view yourself as a rapist?"

"I don't want to think so," he says after awhile. "I want to be something better than that. I don't know what it is, but for years and years I've had this fire in me—that I really enjoy sex, but i was always afraid to confront somebody unless it's sort of like on a businesslike deal. I'll give you this, you do that. But as far as dating somebody or getting to know somebody, it was different." He sighs.

"Frankly, I don't want to spend the rest of my life here. And if I went back out and did what I did again, I'd be right back in here for probably a hundred and fifty years or something like that. I don't want that. Right now, to be honest, I think that if they would let me out on the streets right now, it would probably happen again. Now, why I can't tell you. It's just one of those things. I don't know myself."

I ask Ben whether he has had any psychiatric treatment while in prison.

He looks amused. "No," he states flatly. "I've been working with a social worker, and we've been talking about these problems. They'll give me a few books to read. They started me out on Sigmund Freud. But after the first chapter of the book I just throwed it down. I didn't like it. I took it on my own to start studyin' about myself and why I am this way. Because, believe it or not, it scares me. This last incident where the girl started screaming and I stuck my finger in her mouth—you know, that was just one step further into really hurtin' someone. And God knows, I wouldn't want to hurt anybody."

"You feel that you're sick?"

He takes a deep breath. "Yeah," he answers straightforwardly. "Now, the woman I was workin' with was truly good. She really had a good head on her shoulders, and we talked a whole lot. But the subject of sex never really come up, and we was basically gettin' down to the problems of home, beginning from the childhood up to now. She helped me get this book on Sigmund Freud, and I throwed it away. And there was one on hostility, and it talked about how do you control hostility, anxiety, superiority complexes, and stuff like that," he says, clearly unimpressed.

"Why do you think you were so hostile to women?" I ask.

"That's a good question. I don't know. I think that if I was to grab hold of a man and try to rob him or something, or try to kill him, he just might turn the tails on me. And ever since I was a kid—like it started out with my sister—I've had this bad case of the hots for sex. It's been with me ever since. I don't know, but it's scary."

"Did you feel hostile as well as dominant when you raped a woman?" Sally asks.

Long moments pass before he answers.

"No, then again, yes. I've figured something out, like I took after my mother a whole lot. Even a lot of the guys in here say I've got a lot of feminine characteristics. I guess that's why I take after my mother so much. Now, if that's got anything to do with it, I don't know. Just the way my mother was and the way my mother treated me could have brought on something like I did to these other women."

"How do the other inmates treat you?"

He sighs dejectedly. "Well, I don't get bothered very much. There's some guys here that do, but it's really how you carry yourself. Like this is not my first trip into the penitentiary. And I had trouble in the first penitentiary because I was young. You don't get messed with very much. You mind your own business in here, and they mind theirs."

"Were you ever raped in prison?" Sally asks.

Ben looks a bit embarrassed by the question. "No, but I gave a blow job once," he says, laughing nervously.

"Were you forced to do it?"

"It was more fear on my part," he replies.

Sally changes the subject. "Do you believe women ask to be raped?"

"Well, I think the last one, she more or less asked for it. If she didn't want me in her house, she wouldn't have opened the door, 'cause she really didn't know me at all. She opened the door and let me in, and she's wearing a bikini. Well, that's nothing to be wearing around the house when you got a visitor. There's a lot of teasing out there on both sides of the fence. But there's a lot of good people out there too. I can't answer that. I don't know."

We have been talking for almost an hour now, and it's time to bring the interview to a close.

"Before you leave, I want to show you something," Ben says, reaching into a manila envelope he has brought with him.

"We don't have much time," I say.

"You'll be interested in this," he replies, still fishing through the envelope.

He finally withdraws a piece of paper and hands it to me—some legal document pertaining to his case, I imagine. I peruse it quickly and find instead a letter to Governor Edwin Edwards of Louisiana. It reads as follows.

Dear Sir,

I do not know the correct procedure, chain of command or legal term to write and get an answer from you but . . .

In order for you to understand the purpose of a letter of this caliber, you must be given the background setting. The next paragraph will provide such a setting.

Governor Edwards, I will be the first to admit that over a period of long years I've had emotional problems with myself as well as run-ins with the law. Since the year 1964 until now I've been arrested, jailed, hospitalized for various reasons. I've been everything from an alcoholic to an aggravated rapist. I'm at the point, stage, or verge of institutionalism and I don't want that. I have desperately asked and sought for help without any progress. My record will indicate that. Now I turn to the only man with the power and means to help me. . . .

Governor Edwards, I have made a very important decision in my life based upon Matthew 5:29–30. I have come to the realization as to what is needed for me to become a child of God and a member of our present society. I now send this decision to you with a prayerful request that it can and will be acted upon for an immediate release afterwards. Also I pray that this letter will be examined closely for its sincerity and hope that you will keep this letter classified.

Governor Edwards, it is my decision that I want to undergo an operation that would remove my reproductive organs that would attain my release here from Angola. I would like to speak with you personally on this matter, but if not then the courtesy of a return letter post haste would be greatly appreciated.

I ask if the governor has replied yet, and Ben says no. He also tells me that a copy of the letter was sent to the warden of Louisiana State Penitentiary. We later learned that his request had been denied.

"What good would this kind of operation do?" I ask.

He answers without hesitation. "If I had my organs removed it would get me out of here, and I'd be in a doctor's care. I'm not able to control it." He points to his private parts. "If they take it away from down there—no more problems. I've been doing a lot of thinking about it. It says something about this in the Bible.

"I still have a lot of hostility in me. I feel I'd be serene, more content—I'd lose my sex feelings if I was castrated. I've looked for help. I've been three times in the state hospital. They don't want to counsel or help you. All they want to do is to shoot you up with dope. There's no help here," he continues dejectedly. "There's been times here that I just wanted to be put in the grave. I ain't got the nerve to do it. . . ."

Ray, age 23, was charged with simple rape and was sentenced to ten years at Louisiana State Penitentiary. He served two years of that sentence and went before the parole board in 1980. He was denied parole and has another parole hearing in 1984.

"After your first victim you want to get another one. Maybe she's better-looking or something like that—the way she walks, the way she smiles and talks or something. It gets easier after the first time. Not only easier, it gets more violent. The second, the third, the fourth, the fifth—if I wouldn't have stopped when I got caught, I probably would have killed one of them."

Ray, a soft-spoken, bearded Louisiana native, enters the room and settles comfortably into a chair. He is wearing a blue workshirt, boots, and faded dungarees. Clasping his hands across his stomach, he waits quietly for the interview to begin.

I lead off the questioning. "Tell us about the first time you raped a woman."

113

Ray folds and unfolds his hands as he replies. "It happened at night. It was on a weekend. I was in Lafayette, Louisiana, and I went to a lounge to drink with a friend of mine. We started drinking, and the first thing I knew, about six hours had passed and we're still drinking.

"We happened to meet a lady who was in there, and I started associating with her. First things led to another, and then she wanted to go somewhere else. So she got a car and we took a ride. On the way going down the road, I stopped the car and told her I want to have intercourse with her. She refused me, so I took it upon myself to undress her. After she was undressed I undressed myself and had forceful intercourse with her."

"Did you use a weapon?"

He shakes his head no.

"How did you undress her?"

He sits straight up in his seat. "She struggled, but there was no way she could get me off of her. I'm a big man. She didn't have the same power I did."

"Did she say anything?"

He frowns. "She said, 'No. Why are you doing this?' She never really did me anything. It was just that I was out drinking and the alcohol went to my head. The first thing I knew I had raped a woman."

"How old were you?"

"Eighteen. I was young. She was my first one." He gives me a searching look.

"How many women have you raped?"

"I've raped five times—five women." He averts his eyes.

"When you left the bar with her, were you thinking about rape?"

"No, not at that moment I wasn't," he says, pursing his lips thoughtfully. "I was going on the road with her, and I was goin' somewheres else. I never met this woman before in my life. It was the first time. I was just thinking of having sex with her, but something bounced in my head and said, 'Just do it,' and I did it."

"What bounced into your head? Was it a voice or—"

Ray interrupts, becoming animated. "It's no voice. It's like an evil thing—like the devil is in my mind and your mind tells you to do it."

"Do you think you're possessed by the devil?"

"No, I'm not possessed. If I was, I'd be a vicious man."

114

"After the first rape, did you plan others?"

"Yes, I planned one. She was a juvenile. She was sixteen years old. She had been around town with a few guys I knew over there, and what I did . . ." He pauses. "I happened to spot her one day when she was walking down the road. She was a nice-looking youngster. I started saying to myself I'd like to have her. What I did, I watched where she lived at, and I followed her where she lived, where she would go certain places—this and that—and where she went at night, what time she got back. And when I figured out where was the best spot to get her, I made my attack." Ray looks at Sally, who returns his gaze impassively.

"What was your 'attack' like?" I ask.

He fixes his blue eyes on me. "I didn't really hurt her that much with a knife or things like that. I used my power. I forced her."

"Where did the rape occur?"

"It was in an alley. She'd go down this certain street all the time. I just grabbed her, and I forced her in the alley." He slumps in his chair.

"What did she do?"

"She started screamin' and hollerin'. And the only thing I could do was put my hand over her mouth and keep her from hollerin'. I told her, 'If you don't stop hollerin' I'm gonna hurt you real bad.' She stopped hollerin'. I ripped her clothes off of her. I just forced myself on her."

"Did the girl say anything else?"

"No. She was in shock."

"What went through your mind when you were raping her?"

"I didn't have time to think," he says blankly, clasping and unclasping his hands again. "I just wanted to do something, and I just did it without thinking."

"Was it sexually satisfying to you?"

"Yes, it was."

"How did you feel immediately after the rape?"

"I didn't really feel anything. I just wanted to go and find somebody else, meet some people."

"Did you leave the girl lying in the alley?"

"Yes." His voice is barely audible.

"Was this the rape you were convicted for?"

"No, another one—the last out of five. Three were scared to go to court to testify, I guess, or they didn't want to get involved in front of everyone."

"Did you previously know all the women you raped?"

"I knew a few of them. I had known one or two from a year and a half to five years."

"How did the women react?"

"They were scared to death, scared to death of me," he replies, almost sounding proud of the power he once wielded.

"When you were following the sixteen-year-old, did you consider yourself a rapist?"

"Not really. I just told myself I wanted to rape this girl. I did."

"Did you ever consider asking a woman you were attracted to out for a date?"

"No." He falls silent.

"Why not?"

"I don't know. I can't answer that. If I would have tried I probably could have. At the time I just wanted her, and I took her."

"How do you feel right now about having raped?"

"I feel . . . real low-down. Like I'm nothing." He speaks haltingly. "I feel . . . like I'm nothing at all. I feel worse than a dog or something."

"How do you deal with such feelings?" Sally asks.

He looks at her solemnly. "By getting into all kinds of activities, like social clubs or football, baseball—something like that. And I've been studying the Bible."

"What about psychiatric help?"

He seems amused by the question. "There isn't anybody to talk to. I just keep it inside and say nothin'. I just try to better myself. When I first came here it was worse. I was bad on myself. Like every day I'd walk around and start thinking to myself about all these things I've done to all these women, why I did it. There was no reason for doin' it. It was something that happened."

I press him. "There must have been some reason for doing it."

"There was some reason, but—" He breaks off abruptly. "I was married for three years. I had a son. She was a beautiful wife and everything. I had my wife at home when I went down the street to look for a victim. And when I found her I used her."

"When you raped these women, did you also sodomize them?" I ask.

He stares past me. "They blew me, and one of them, I shoved a fist up her cunt. This one I screwed from behind."

"Those are pretty violent acts, don't you think?"

116

"I didn't lay my hand on them and slap them around," he says defensively. "I didn't slice them or nothin' like that—slice her up with a knife or shoot her or somethin' like that."

"Where did all that violence come from?"

Ray shifts uncomfortably in his chair, his eyes wandering around the room. "I don't know. I really don't know."

"Were you violent with your wife?"

"Yes, I was." He crosses and uncrosses his legs.

"What kind of things did you do?"

"Raping her, sticking my fist up her cunt."

"Were you sexually satisfied at home?"

He nods. "It was just that sometimes my wife and I would have a bad trip, a bad going between ourselves. She'd get angry, and I'd get angry, and we'd start a fight. First thing I knew, I was out on the street riding around in my car or something. I was looking for somebody to take it out on or something like that. I've hurt my wife before . . . many times."

"Were any of the rapes sparked by your arguments at home?"

"Yes, maybe one or two. See, we'd start arguin' over nothing, really, and she'd get me so mad I'd want to hit her—I'd want to beat her up. Instead, I'd just walk out the house. I'd go take me a walk somewhere or get in my car. And I'd get ridin' down the road, and I'd spot somebody. And the thing started comin' in my head sayin', 'Well, this girl looks nice, I'd like to have her.' The first thing I knew, I was watchin' her and this and that—you know. After some time had passed by I attacked her."

"You followed her?"

"Yeah, I'd follow her by car all around. Sometimes I'd get out of my car and walk around, follow her uptown where she was goin'. And when I saw she'd get in her car, I'd follow her to her house, a friend's house, wherever she was goin'."

"Did you single out any particular type of woman?"

"Not really. I'd rape any woman."

"Even elderly women?"

He shakes his head no.

"Is there anything you can remember that might have caused you to become a rapist?" Sally asks.

Long moments pass as he thinks about the question. "Well," he finally says, "let me say how I think it really started is that it happened way back in my childhood. I was—I'd say nine or ten years old. I saw my father do the same thing to my mother." A pained expression clouds his features. "He raped her with a Coke bottle. He used his hand on her and this and that. As I'm growin' up, you know, I still had this on my mind. My father left my mother when I was fourteen, and I've been living with her ever since. I guess that's what started me rapin'. From the violence I saw from my father—what he did to my mother."

"It would seem that what your father did would turn you off to men rather than women."

"Right. It did. I wouldn't mess with a man. I wouldn't associate with them."

"How's your relationship with your mother?"

He smiles gently. "We get along real great. Whatever she needs I get for her, and she'd do the same for me."

"You said you wouldn't associate with men because of what your father did to your mother?"

"Right. This was all built up in my head. I was angry at my father. Being angry at him, being he was a man, I was angry at men. What I couldn't do to them, I would take it out on a woman."

"But why not take it out on a man?" Sally asks.

Ray avoids the question. "You'd have to be there to really see what happened. He was doin' this to my mother, and all the agony and everything she was goin' through—it would stay in my head." He pauses, seeming preoccupied by grim reflections. "So when I was old enough and I would go out, I would look for a victim. And when I'd find her I'd do the same things he did—see the expression on their face, all the yells and screams. Never did use a Coke bottle, though. I used my fist."

"When did all this start happening?"

"When I was about eighteen."

"And how long did it continue?"

"Maybe . . . four years. Four years I was doing this, maybe once or twice a week or something like that." He sounds angry.

"Why would you transfer that violence to women?" I ask.

This time he answers without hesitation. "It was like he was learnin' me something and I was small and I didn't know any better. He didn't really try to learn me anything better than what I saw. As I grew up with it, it got worse and worse, and I wanted to do it myself. When I was eighteen I had one of my own. That's when I first tried it."

"How do you feel about women in general?"

He smiles. "I see women as strong as other people—as a

118

man—not weak. They're a lot better-looking, and some of them are smarter."

"Do you think women ask to be raped?" Sally wants to know.

"Some of them do. Some of them walk around with short-shorts, you know, showing their body off. And because they're good-looking, some of them, they walk around with no bra underneath. And you see a woman walking down the street like that, and you look at her. What it does, it just starts a man to thinking that if he gets something like this, what he can do with it."

"How would you suggest that women dress?"

"With a dress. Something underneath it. With a bra on."

"What type of woman do you find attractive?"

Ray smiles again. "I liked one that was free with herself. She likes to get involved sexually or otherwise. I'd like for her to have a head on her shoulders—you know, some smarts in her. She has to have a nice personality. She has to look good, of course."

"What would have turned you off from committing those rapes?"

"It's hard to say. I would have done anything to a woman at that time."

"What if they were in great pain?"

He frowns. "They was in great pain. I just laughed in their face. I thought it was a joke. It was a good feeling to me."

"Why was it a good feeling?"

"Why? I don't know. I guess it goes back to my childhood, when I'd seen my father do the same thing to my mother."

"But your mother must've looked like she was in great pain," Sally pursues.

He shrugs. "She was. She suffered a lot."

"If a woman encouraged you to rape her, would that have put you off?"

"No."

"When will you get out of prison?"

"This year, I hope."

"Will your attitude towards women be any different when you get out of here?"

He nods vigorously. "Yes, it's changed a lot. It changed over the time I've been locked up. I look at a woman more respectfully now."

"Are you through raping women?"

He laughs. "Yes, I sure am. The sentence I'm doin' right now is hard. It's hard to be away from people."

119

"Would you like to meet your victims again?"

"Yes."

"What would you say?"

He smiles wanly. "What can you say, really, except that you're sorry? It's the only thing you can say. But there's nothing you can do but try to make them forget about that it happened. And it'll always stay with them for the rest of their lives."

"Did raping leave you with any psychological scars?" I ask.

"It sure did. It sure did," he says gravely.

"How do you define a rapist?"

"A rapist is a wild person. He's sick. He has only one thing on his mind, and that's a woman. He wants that woman. He wants to have intercourse with her no matter how he gets it or where he gets it. He has something wrong with him, a mental problem where he was brought up like that or something."

"Do you view yourself as this type of rapist?"

"When I first came here I did. Now I don't."

"Do you think about raping women when you masturbate?" Sally wants to know.

"I sure don't," he replies emphatically.

"But you used to?"

"Oh, yes. Every night and during the day when I'd be walking along, I'd have fantasies about raping women. I'd be thinking of the things I'd be doin' to them."

"Which rape are you in here for?"

"This one which got me locked up, she was related to a city policeman. He's the one that put me in here. She went to bed with my brother one night, and she had intercourse with him. Her husband was in the service. She was living with herself and a little baby. She sent this guy over to get in touch with my brother and tell him she wanted to sleep with him—she wanted to meet him, that's what it was.

"Later that night he went over to her house, knocked on her door. She came to the door and offered him to come in. So he goes in and stays with her all that night and comes back the next morning. We talked about it. I asked him how she was in bed and all this and that, what she really liked. So he told me. So I took it upon myself, I was going to go myself. And that's what I did.

"I went over to her house. She was walking around in some shorts and a low-cut blouse. Her little baby was in the bed sleeping. I started lookin' around the house through a window to watch what

120

she was doing. I knocked on the door, and she opened it and she saw it was me. She didn't try to shut the door or scream or nothing, she just asked me what I wanted. I told her I'd like to come in, I'd like to talk to her for a minute. And she knew me at that time. She'd been ignoring me all her life practically. So she asked me what I wanted to talk about, and at the same time I shoved the door open.

"I walked in there and shut the door. I grabbed her, and I brought her to the bedroom. I took her clothes off, and I told her I was going to rape her. She put up a little struggle, but she was too weak to handle me. I overpowered her. We got into bed, and I told her, 'If you don't do what I want you to do, I'm gonna kill you and your baby.' And the first thing she's gonna look out for is her child. She don't want her child harmed. She did what I wanted her to do.

"I *fucked* her. I shoved my fist in her. She turned around, and I had intercourse from the back. After I was through she was just laying there. I put my clothes back on, and I left. I lived only maybe a couple of blocks away from her. So I went inside my house and laid down by the side of my wife like nothin' had happened. I went to sleep.

"The next morning her uncle, who was chief of detectives on the police force, knocked on my door. He said I was arrested for aggravated rape. They picked me up, and I was brought to jail. I was facing life at the time—ninety-nine years. But they dropped the charges from aggravated rape to simple rape."

"Do you think you wanted to be caught?" Sally asks.

"I must've wanted to get caught because of the way I went about things. I had raped a few women before that. When you start rapin' you don't think. You don't think at all. All you want to do is attack that victim and get it over with. When it's done, you can say that's one more that you raped. It's mostly anger that you feel. What you're doing is taking out that anger on her."

"You said to yourself, 'That's one more that I raped.' Is it like keeping a scorecard?"

"It's not like keeping a scorecard. It's just seeing how many you can rape, you know, before you get caught."

"Did you rape because you felt sexually inadequate?"

"No," he replies after a long pause. "I raped five women in my time. When I get out I hope to God I don't have to do that no more—I hope I'm all right. I've been thinking that the next time if

121

I do it, it's the end of it for me. It makes the third time I've been arrested for the same charge. After the third time you go to the penitentiary for life. That's why I'm trying to better myself."

"Is it the fear of returning to prison that will keep you straight?" I ask.

He looks me squarely in the eyes. "Yes, it's the fear. Now, a man sits back and thinks about all the things he did—fine, it's all over with. Now he has to face what's ahead of him. If he doesn't better himself, hell, he'll be right back here again."

"How did your wife react when she found out what you'd done?"

"She couldn't believe it. She knew I did it to her several times. She couldn't believe I done it to another woman."

"Did your wife divorce you?"

He nods silently.

"Why did you have to rape your wife?"

"She wasn't giving it to me when I wanted it," he says bitterly. "Three or four times a week I would want to have intercourse. Maybe once a week she would want to. What I would do is take it upon myself and force her to do it. . . ." His voice trails off and he falls silent.

"Try to describe what it feels like being a rapist."

He furrows his brow. "You see, you have to be a rapist to know. After your first victim you want to get another one. Maybe she's better-looking or something like that—the way she walks, the way she smiles and talks or something. It gets easier after the first time. Not only easier, it gets more violent. The second, the third, the fourth, the fifth—if I wouldn't have stopped when I got caught, I probably would have killed one of them."

"So maybe you sensed that on the last one?"

He nods. "I knew what I was doin' at the time I was doin' it. Something just told me, 'You rapin', you hurtin' women, slap 'em around, this and that, you know. What's the next one going to be like? Are you going to kill them or not?'"

"Why did you become more violent?"

"Whenever you're raping a woman, it's the things you're doing to her that gets you excited," he says, staring at his hands. "You go berserk. You try something more or harder to use on her, like a fist or a Coke bottle—that's what it is."

"So you think you would've ended up killing one of your victims eventually?"

"Yes, I would. I sure would've."

122

Dave, age 25, served two years of a five-year sentence at Louisiana State Penitentiary for attempted forcible rape. He was paroled in 1979.

"So I broke a bottle. . . . I held it to her throat and got on top of her. . . . I ate her and tried to get her to suck me off, but she wouldn't do it. It kinda made me mad, but I wasn't gonna make her physically do something—because, like I say, my mother didn't bring me up that way to hurt a woman."

Dave enters the room and rolls up the sleeves of his workshirt.

"You know what these are from?" he demands, displaying his wrists. He gives both of us a hard stare. "I wanted to kill myself because of what I done. These scars I got here—I cut myself. I was gonna cut the other side another time, but an old convict that was up in the jailhouse stopped me. He said it wasn't worth it." His eyes scan our faces, searching for a response.

123

THE RAPIST FILE

"You mean you tried to kill yourself twice because of the rapes you committed?" I ask.

"Yes. I figured I had enough Satan in my heart that I would go back out there and do this again."

Dave is a solidly built man with curly brown hair and a small mustache. Under his workshirt he wears a white T-shirt with a pair of sunglasses clipped to the V neck. His eyes have a glazed, inwardly focused expression, and his smile reveals two crooked rows of gapped teeth. He speaks softly and has a tendency to stutter slightly.

"Tell us something about your background," I say.

"I grew up in the country, in Texas, and from seven to fourteen I lived in the city. My parents, they didn't get along too well, and my dad, he was an alcoholic, and he was pussy-whipped." His eyes flicker with disdain. "He and my mom had a few falling-outs, and they ended up getting a divorce. I had a younger brother than me, and my mom had to take care of him. My father wasn't payin' no child support or nothin', so I told her I'd make it on my own at fourteen." He drums on the table continuously as he speaks.

"So I left home, and I've been on my own ever since. And I went and worked around horses and livestock, and from there I went into the service. So I came back out of the service in '73—I only stayed in the service maybe a year and a month, 'cause they wouldn't let me stay overseas. They wanted to send me back to Norfolk, Virginia. I didn't like that place, so I got out on a drug exemption. 'Cause I've done some drugs in my time. And from then on I've been hitchhiking around, more or less."

Dave extracts a plastic cigarette lighter from his pants pocket and lights up. He continues to play with it as he discusses his life. "I didn't start thinkin' about chicks until I went back home, and what burns me up sometimes about chicks is dick-teasers. They lead a man on and then shut him off right there. I guess that's what made me just go ahead and forcibly take it. My mother raised me different. She raised me to respect my elders and stuff like that. I wouldn't have normally done that if I wasn't drunk and all speeded up.

"It was one of my girlfriend's best friends, this woman I had raped. My girlfriend had left the bar early that night, and her girlfriend came lookin' for her at this bar where I hung around. This was in Abbeville, Louisiana. And so I told her my girlfriend went home, and she stayed at the bar drinkin'.

"So I had a lot of money on me—about four hundred dollars—so I was buyin' the rounds at the bar and all that. And I had bought some Valiums and some other drugs. My girlfriend's about three hundred pounds, and she gets those diet pills, you know, so I always have those. So it gets about two o'clock and the bar's closin', so we had to leave. That's when I told her I'd take her home." He breaks off.

"I'm sidetrackin'. I'm gonna have to go back into the story a little bit more. See, I always looked at her in a lustful way. Did stuff for her when my chick should have seen through it, but she didn't. I bought her pizzas and carried her to the store. I never went through that with my own girlfriend.

"So while we was at the bar I kept throwin' these pills in her beer, and she never did notice it. I guess I was tryin' to knock her out or get her head really spaced out. So we started walkin' home, and I put my arm around her, and I was doin' things in my head about her. I guess I was tryin' a slick con on her—I don't know. So instead of me takin' her home, I went and took her to the dump where I used to drive a dump truck at. And I couldn't raise a hard-on 'cause of that speed. I'd been takin' it so long that it messed up my body." He laughs humorlessly.

"So she says, 'Quit now, and I won't call rape. If you keep on I'm gonna call it rape.' I didn't tear no clothes or I didn't hit her—I only hit a couple of chicks in my life. I thought somehow that maybe I'd build something inside, so I busted a bottle. I didn't have to have the bottle, because I done had all her clothes off without bustin' the bottle, but I guess I was doin' something with my male ego. It didn't work. It still didn't work. So I held it to her throat and got on top of her, and it still didn't work. So I threw it way out in a field maybe ten or fifteen feet away. The cops never did find it. . . ." He pauses.

"I'm the one that ratted on myself. She left town two days after it happened. But anyway, I ate her and tried to get her to suck me off, but she wouldn't do it. It kinda made me mad, but I wasn't gonna make her physically do something—because, like I say, my mother didn't bring me up that way to hurt a woman. I can turn around and kill a man a hell of a lot quicker."

"What was this girl saying to you while all this was going on?" I ask.

"She was shuck-shuck."

"What?"

"She was shuck-shuck—cryin'. You know what I mean? By

shuck-shuck—she was cryin' a little bit. That's what I couldn't figure out, 'cause usually when a girl's getting eaten she's digging it. But this chick wasn't digging it. She says, 'Please stop, please stop. What am I going to say to Hilda?' Hilda's my girlfriend.

"My mind was so spaced out that I just acted like she was a rag doll. I talked to her every now and then"—he stammers—"and she kept on sayin', 'Take me home, take me home.' And finally I told her, 'Here's the goddamn truck. Get in it and leave. Just get in it and leave. I don't care how I make it back.' But she wouldn't do that."

"Why?"

He shrugs. "I don't know. It was peculiar as hell to me. When I told her that, it broke us up, and I went to the truck." He pauses, then resumes without prompting. "Dope don't fall back on rape or nothing like that. I don't think it does, because if a person's gonna rape somebody, he's got it in his head. He's gonna do it, or it's planned out. And I had planned this rape out in my head, but I never"—again he stammers—"fulfilled it. Because to me somebody that rapes a girl is the lowest thing on God's green earth."

"Why do you think that?"

"Because it's taking advantage of a weak person," he says firmly. "Just like these punks that come here in the penitentiary, and they're weak 'cause of their size. And a dude takes advantage of 'em. I can't see that. I look out for one over at the camp, but I don't let him know that—I mean, he knows it shuck-shuck—but I stopped two or three niggers from trying to rape him. It's just the strong survive and the weak perish."

"How did you feel about the rape right afterwards?"

"I wanted to kill myself. I took her home, and I said, 'Don't call Hilda. Do me a favor and don't call Hilda.' I had a hundred dollars. I gave her a hundred dollars, and I said, 'Give this to Hilda.' She says, 'Why? What are you gonna do?' I said, 'I'm gonna kill myself.'"

"So you turned yourself in?"

"I ratted on myself more or less. I took 'em to the place where it happened. I guess I had a guilty conscience."

"So she did call the cops?"

He nods. "I dropped her home about three-thirty, so I kept her out for about an hour and a half. So I dropped her off and gave her that bread. I left her, and I was gonna go by my girlfriend's house to see if her light was on. That way I knew if her light was on she

126

called her, 'cause my girlfriend didn't stay up 'til no three-thirty in the morning.

"So anyway, I was going down the street, and I run a stoplight, so they started chasin' me. So I was tryin' to make it towards Crowley, and I done have it in my head that I was gonna kill myself somehow. So I made it across this bridge, and I decided right then to turn the truck around. I turned the truck around in the middle of the road, and the cops stopped on the bridge. They freaked out. I guess they thought I was gonna ram them or something.

"Anyway, I drove the truck off the bridge. The engine landed in the river, but the body of the truck landed on the bank. So I jumped out into the water and swam under the water on my back. I made it to the pilings until the sun started comin' up and they was fishin' for my body. They thought I had drowned. So I made it up on top. They done went down the river—down the current—lookin' for me. They thought I had drowned." He grins.

"I walked around tryin' to get back to this house I was rentin' at. When I got back, this landlady, she tells me, she says, 'Look, the cops are looking for you.' She tried to cover up for me, but the cops saw me come inside the house. I was up there in the attic hiding. But when they said something about a search warrant, I come down so I wouldn't drag that little old lady into it.

"They put me in this itty-bitty room in the city jailhouse, and I heard this girl talkin'. I don't know if they brought her down to identify me or not. That cell I was in had a little hole in it, but I couldn't see out. That's when I figured right there that she's comin' to rat on me now.

"So they took me into another room in the police station and gave me all my rights and that bull. I think they were just runnin' down a tip on me. But at that point I had already come down off that speed, and I was feelin' ashamed of myself for what I had done. I just started copping out to 'em with a tape recorder in front of me and everything. I told 'em where it happened, took 'em to where it happened." His shoulders sag, and he shakes his head disgustedly.

"You say you don't know what made you do it?" Sally asks.

He gropes absently for his lighter. "I like big titties, like Dolly Parton. I drool over her. But that's what kicks it off. That's what kicks my head off. It starts me thinkin' she's got some pretty nice knockers. I start planning and scheming in my little head, and I didn't start doing this until about three years ago."

"What started it all?"

"I guess it all started with this chick in Texas. She was a prick-teaser." He eyes Sally. "I raped her just like the chick in Abbeville, but this time I got my enjoyment out of it." His stammer erupts more frequently now. "She'd go so far with a dude, and she'd shut him off right there. I was dealin' some drugs, and I met her at a party. I turned her on to some mescaline and stuff like that, and I met her brothers and all that. So I talked her into taking me home. Before this I busted a wine bottle and had the neck. So when we started drivin' I brought up the question let's go get a lid, and she said yeah. I said I knew a place on such and such a road.

"So we started ditty-bopping out there, and I pulled over to the side of the road. She says, 'What you doing?' And then I put the bottle up to her throat, and she was scared. And she didn't give me no trouble or nothing, and I took her out there. And she got to enjoyin' it and never did cry. She ate me first, and then I screwed her and she played with my ass. About all that came out of that was a fight with her brothers."

"You said you decided three years ago to start raping women?"

"Yeah, I guess I did in a way because—I don't know. I just like big titties. I really didn't decide it three years ago. I was thinkin' about it heavy three years ago. But since I've been in Abbeville, that's when I started schemin'—well, I know this chick and I know that chick, and I'm gonna plan something with them."

"Do you feel you need psychiatric help?"

"Yes, but I don't want to because I might make that parole. But if I don't make that parole, I would. This penitentiary, though, it ain't got no psychiatric help."

"What does asking about psychiatric help have to do with your parole?"

He laughs. "Hell, you ask to see a shrink, and they use that against you. Say you're crazy and stay locked up."

Sally changes the subject. "Do you feel women ask to be raped?"

He gives her a crooked grin. "Yeah, by dick-teasing. By puttin' 'em off. It's the way they talk that's got a lot to do with it."

"What kind of talk?"

"Perverted talk. 'Well, I fucked that dude' or something like that—you know." Now he sounds angry.

"Did you feel powerful when you raped?" I ask.

"Yeah," he almost croons. "I felt like I had everything in the world. I could do what I wanted. When you rape these women—I really can't explain it—it makes your male ego really souped up. Like if you had Superman powers, you know? But after it was over I felt ashamed of myself that I did enjoy it."

"Do you think if you get out you'll rape again?"

"It depends on what kind of crowd I hang around with. If I get back in that dope crowd and my mind starts gettin' spaced out again, I know I will. But if I stay back home—East Texas—where I can stay around my mom and look after my mom shuck-shuck, she'll snap me back to reality."

"The rape where you said you enjoyed it—did you hold the bottle on her all the time?"

"No, I laid the bottle down. She could have jigged me with it if she wanted to. I mean, she was scared, you could see that. And at first she said, 'I don't want to.' And that's when I held it closer, and then she said okay." He smiles.

I tell him that the interview time is up.

"I had something else in mind about this." Dave remains seated, rolling down his sleeves.

"Like what?"

"I got religion now. I found religion. . . ."

Quentin, age 33, has served five years of a seven-and-a-half-year sentence for simple rape at Louisiana State Penitentiary. He went before the parole board in 1979 and was denied parole. His good-time discharge date is August 26, 1981.

"I had this image of being the Don Juan when I would be with a woman. I figured if I could overpower her sexually, then plus my sexual gratification, I was accomplishing an ego thing where they'd want to see me again."

Quentin is a perfect specimen of the Joe College type—tall, blond, blue-eyed, the all-American boy next door, voted by his classmates Most Likely to Succeed. Everything about him fosters this impression—his clean-cut, collegiate appearance, the thoughtful manner in which he couches his replies to questions, the bright look in his eyes. With his Southern charm and magnetic personality, he is quite disarming.

Quentin has carved the perfect niche for himself at Louisiana

131

State Penitentiary. His nickname is Lawyer, and he is precisely that—a self-taught jailhouse legal expert who has made himself almost as valuable to the inmates as the keys to the prison would be. Quentin reviews their legal briefs, helps them write letters to their attorneys, coaches them on their rights, and generally acts as combination ombudsman and advocate for the prison population. As a result, he is a popular and widely respected figure among inmates, and a thorn in the side of prison officialdom.

Quentin is in particularly high spirits this morning, and with good reason. After three years in prison, he is due before the parole board in a matter of weeks. And then, he tells us, he has special plans in mind.

"I've had an offer to work with the Southern Prisoner Coalition and try to organize some prison reform committees—that type of thing," he says enthusiastically. "We're working on something through the district attorney's office out of Baton Rouge."

"What kind of thing?"

A smile flits across his face. "It's quite heavy. It's called Women Against Rape or something like that. What we're trying to achieve there is to have some type of communication level where we could actually go to the street and visit college students—any female from the age of like sixteen up—and let them know the situation or circumstances that they can be put into, and complications they can expect in a rape situation if they don't know the person they're with."

"You mean you're going to be lecturing to women on college campuses about rape?"

Quentin nods. "More or less of an awareness thing," he adds. "To be aware of what your surroundings are, what's going on—always to be aware of where you're at. The area I'm more or less planning on lecturing on pertains to freshmen college women in situations where they're from a small town and have moved to a large community where they're not used to the bar scene. They're not used to involvement with the drug scene that's happening on campus and the type of male that they would run into that would have sexual intentions. Maybe he wouldn't have the intention to rape at the first meeting, but which would develop after being around them in relationship to being in a bar. How to be aware of it, what to look out for—the overfriendliness thing.

"The overfriendliness thing," he repeats. "The sexual indications on the first meeting, like 'I've seen you before, I've watched

132

you before,' and that type of thing. As if the guy has been aware of her presence even though she hasn't been aware of him. If it's a situation where she meets a guy in a bar, then I'll be speaking basically from personal experience. I'll be trying to go into where situations have developed in my personal background—where if she meets a guy in a bar, if she's with a group of people, not to leave the group of people, or at least let them be aware of his presence and identification. That type of thing, in case the situation developed where she was missed for any length of time."

It seems a solid piece of advice, coming as it does from a man whose record of arrests for rape stretches back almost ten years, to his freshman year at Memphis State University.

"Was there a particular type of woman that attracted you?" Sally asks.

"It's hard to say." Quentin absently scratches his head. "Generally, in my situation, I've had rapport with women that has not always involved rape. I've had an extremely heavy sexual background—everything, in fact, from the ages of sixteen to sixty. She was the oldest woman I've ever been to bed with." His eyes flicker with private amusement.

"As far as the rape thing goes, it's a preference for something that would be more or less the Hollywood movie star, the really flashy type of female. And this is something the woman needs to notice—her dress. If it's very seductive, if a guy has a problem in his mental makeup, it's a type of come-get-me thing. It's an alluring effect."

He furrows his brow in concentration. "It's not so much that you've got to go around with a sack over your head all the time. If you're going to be involved with people that you've never met—for the first time going to a bar, for example—or if you're in a crowd of people at a concert, the thing is to try to tone down your sexual appeal until you can become familiar with your surroundings or until you start picking people's faces up."

"Do you think women have to be wary of strange men all the time?" I ask.

He nods. "I think there's a lot of imbalance in males. I'm speaking in the area of colleges, because this is my background. A guy coming from a protected home, or a guy coming even from a broken home situation, has a lot of things he wants vented through raping a woman. He may feel sexual frustration with females or something. A female needs to be paranoid."

133

THE RAPIST FILE

"Do you think women are being fed misinformation about rapists?" Sally asks.

Quentin grins at the question. "Sure. They're seeing them jumping out of trees, behind bushes, comin' up out of the back of cars. In the last five or ten years this, it seems, is what has really been brought to the public's eyes. But it's the everyday guy you wouldn't really suspect—the bank teller, the nice guy, the eight-to-five guy who holds a job. Those people have more tendency to be latent rapists than anybody to my knowledge, and it's been discussed in length with different people—fraternity brothers, college professors, whatever, guys that I have known personally that could be potential rapists.

"There needs to be exposure from the rapist himself instead of someone trying to present the rapist image and not have any first-hand knowledge themselves, not being a rapist. From what I understand about the Baton Rouge thing, the district attorney's wife is head of the rape crisis program. From my understanding, she's never been a rape victim. So how can she have this knowledge other than statistical facts? This can really be presented in the wrong image. It's a misconception, I feel."

"Are you saying that most of the rapists in this prison are the nice, everyday people you just described?"

"A few of the guys that have been in here for quite a length of time—I'm speaking of the black guys mainly—they've had some pretty bizarre, perverted acts involving the crime itself. I think a lot of it is glorified from the actual situation—things they've dreamed up in their heads."

"In an actual rape situation, what are you going to tell women to do? Struggle or not struggle?" Sally asks.

"It depends on how they value their life. If their moral ethics are to the point where they feel that the act itself would deflower them or ruin them for the rest of their life, they're going to of course fight. In that situation you don't know what the rapist is like. It might scare him. He might kill you.

"If I would suggest anything, first of all be as calm as possible, and if there can be any conversation had—if you can get this guy talking to you—you've got half the battle won right there. If it's a situation where it's a real rough, abrupt act and there's no communication, that should be your first indication to just go ahead and submit to the act and try to save your ass. You can't pick a path. If the guy's action is this, you react this way. You never really know."

134

"How will you feel as a former rapist sitting in an audience crowded with women?" I ask.

"As if I'm a sick, deranged individual and this is my scarlet letter for the rest of my life?" he retorts rhetorically. "Personally, I don't have that insight into the thing," he says after a pause. "What I feel more so is that the situation here in the penitentiary is that they suppress anything as far as trying to get this out of your system—to try to talk about it, the counseling aspect. To me, more or less the obligation that I owe—if you have to pay back society— is that this would be paying society back by the exposure. Plus it's goin' to work twofold. It's goin' to take a lot of frustration and vent a lot of frustration that I have, that could possibly at a later time— right circumstances, right situation—could possibly happen again. A heavy alcoholic background, financial problems, that type of thing, could make it happen again."

We now turn from the subject of Quentin's future plans and ask him to tell us something about his background.

"My father's a retired lieutenant colonel in the Air Force. I have a brother with a degree, a sister with a degree; my mother's older sister is a psychologist here in the state of Louisiana. There's a heavy educational background throughout the whole family on both sides. Financially, we're very stable on my father's side. On my mother's side, they've always worked for a living, that kind of thing. Everything they've got they've had to struggle for, but now they're reaping the benefits in their elder age or whatever." He pauses for a moment, then continues in a soft voice.

"I think the problem developed when I was eleven years old and my parents were divorced. I went with my mother and younger brother." Quentin begins to rock in his chair nervously as the conversation becomes more personal. "The situation with my mother and I was an overprotection thing at first—I could say a six-year period throughout the later part of elementary school, all through junior high school and the freshman year in high school.

"I think she was trying to shelter a lot of things that my dad had done within the marriage that was being brought to my attention by other family members—that is, drinking, and he had numerous women friends. He was a pilot and had all these super affairs all over the country. This was always being brought up. I idolized my dad. I thought it was pretty far-out to be able to have all these women all over the country and still be able to maintain the family image that he did for so many years prior to the divorce."

135

Quentin continues to rock in his seat. "It had its effects in so much as when I was in high school or even freshman year in college, there was a lot of frustration that developed beause of the relationship that I had with my mother and the people she would bring to the house. It would be a lot of secretaries she worked with, women that would be anywhere from about six to twelve years older than I. And there was a lot of kidding—you know, 'If he was a little older . . .' and that kind of stuff. It built a lot of fantasies up. I think this is where the rapist thing started developing."

"Could resentment towards your mother also have been a contributing factor?"

He shakes his head no. "Not so much that it brought anything to the surface. If anything, I think it brought a compassion for the victim because of the protection that my mother had given me for so many years."

"In what ways was your mother overprotective?"

He looks somber. "Staying away from the wrong side of town, that kind of stuff. This was one of her biggest objections was hanging around with the wrong kind of crowd. And the right girl, that was brought in a couple of times. I had a crush on a girl who got pregnant from the preacher's son of the church we attended. And there was a question that I might have been involved in it. That was really, I think, the only ill feeling I had toward my mother was the suppression of that. Because I really had a crush on this girl."

"Did you ever entertain any violent feelings towards women?"

He shakes his head vigorously. "None. Not so much in a physical thing where I'm going to chop her head off or shoot 'em or cut 'em. As far as the rape thing, the frustration that I released was in the sexual act itself. I had this image of being the Don Juan when I would be with a woman. I figured if I could overpower her sexually, then plus my sexual gratification, I was accomplishing an ego thing where they'd want to see me again."

"Did raping make you feel powerful?"

He smiles. "Extremely so. I had the Big Man on Campus image for a couple of years."

"How did you feel when you made love to a woman you didn't rape?" Sally asks.

"It was more of an act," he says thoughtfully. "It was more of just a play instead of an expression. It was the stallion effect. I knew what I was supposed to be—this is the reputation, and you should be on your knees because of the fact that I'm even here with you."

"Do you think most men want to rape?" Sally asks.

"It's like saying does everybody have a little homosexual in them. I'd say yes—right circumstances, under the right pressure or whatever, it could be very easy to subject a woman to rape."

"Conversely, do you think every woman wants to be raped?"

"It's hard to say every woman, because it's an area where there's so much morality involved—now more so, with the sexual thing being flaunted. My personal feelings are that there's a lot of fantasy involved. I'd say a lot of women probably would. Probably not so much the violent act itself, but maybe the lover they never had. If it was an act of rape, they could play it off as something else—a fantasy."

"How did you go about committing a rape?" Sally asks.

Quentin takes a deep breath. "Generally by drinking. The crime that I'm here on was that I met a girl at a disco. She said that she'd seen me there before and noticed me. And when she said that I immediately knew that this was going to be another jump-in-the-sack situation. As it turned out, her hesitancy brought the rape on. At one point there was an agreement that we were going to have sex. But then it seemed—I don't know—like we both sobered up and she became aware of where she was at, who she was with, and that I wasn't her fiancé.

"She came from a very religious, moral background, and she snapped and went completely cold. And when she went that, I went the complete reverse. She's a very small woman. She's about five foot three and weighed about one hundred and ten pounds. I'm six one and weigh two hundred and five pounds, so it was no problem at all in respect to forcing her.

"Her bra was off—I'd taken that off. I'd had some foreplay with her. It just consisted of taking her pantyhose and underwear off and laying on top of her. At one point she did scream, and I raised up off her and looked at her. She started crying. That's when the rape was committed."

"You didn't care about her protestations?"

"Not then. The sexual thing was in mind, and that was the whole thing. I felt that if I could get inside her physically and start my performance, that would circumvent whatever problems we had. As it turned out, it just multiplied them." He laughs bitterly.

"Afterwards I had a lot of remorse. In fact, immediately after we were even talking about it. And she had more sense about her than I did. This may sound petty, but I was crying. It wasn't so

137

much a forgive-me thing as that I had snapped to what had happened—the act itself constituted a rape."

"Is this when you first thought of yourself as a rapist?"

"That's when I first knew I could commit the act. There was no power involved. I felt like a little kid that just got his hand slapped."

"But that wasn't the first woman you raped, right?"

He nods.

"So did you anywhere along the line view yourself as a rapist, or did you just think of yourself as a good lover?"

He shrugs. "More so a good lover than jumping out of a tree. It's always in a situation where the question is whether or not we're going to have sex. And if they say no, it's usually I say yes, and it ends up the act is committed."

"When did you commit your first rape?"

Quentin is ready with the details. "This is when I was a freshman in college—Memphis State University. The lady was an economics teacher. I played tennis with her, and this is how the relationship evolved. Her husband quit playing doubles with us, and I was seeing one of these Mrs. Robinson things coming on."

He resumes his rocking. "Her complete understanding was that I was nothing more than a nice-guy student. I was having all these fantasies that this was going to be my older-woman-all-through-college type thing. What happened was that I was in a fraternity at the time, and they had a rush week. She had brought a friend of her husband's over to the fraternity house. There was some drinking involved, and we left in her car and went to a place called Overton Park. This is when I started telling her all these feelings that I had towards her. And it completely blew her mind. She had no idea that this was goin' on. I forced myself on her, started kissin' her. The force involved was holding her back. And then, after awhile, my belief now is that she knew she was about to be raped. That is why she just completely submitted to it."

"What happened afterwards?"

"She went home, told her husband, and he came over and said he was going to castrate me, beat my balls off and all this kind of stuff. One of the fraternity brothers at the house had to restrain him. And they called the cops. Her husband explained to them what the situation was, and they went to her house, took a statement, and came back and arrested me."

"Did the woman press charges?"

"No, there were no charges filed at all."

"Was that close call enough to deter you from raping again for awhile?"

Quentin nods. "Seven years," he says. "Nothing happened in between."

"How long is the sentence you're serving now?"

"Seven and a half years. I've been here since March 1976."

"How are you treated by the guards and other inmates?"

His eyes cloud with anger as he answers. "It's just like any penitentiary, from my understanding. We're the bottom of the barrel, we're the sickos. The guys that commit murder, shoot little kids, and that stuff—they're in the top echelon. And then you have your bank robbers, forgers, that type of thing. And then the rapists. A lot of guys suppress it here. A lot of guys, you think they're burglars. But since I do a lot of legal stuff down here I know their cases. That's my name. They call me Lawyer. Everybody has a little nickname in this place." Quentin grins, then becomes serious as he goes on.

"The security staff is *extremely* prejudiced towards rapists in this place. A white guy, you've got a little chance to breathe. A black rapist—phew! Hang it up. A black rapist who has raped a white woman here, they're still looking at it like the 1950s. A black rapist has a really tough time. You're not allowed to go into trustee status, no matter how your conduct is. In my situation, I've had two write-ups—more or less disciplinary problems. I was reprimanded. There was no cellblock or lock-down action involved." He pauses for a moment.

"I meet every requirement in the world to be classified as a trustee status. But due to the fact that I'm a sex offender, I don't get that status," he says bitterly. "Everybody knows what you're here for. There's no security involved in trying to keep records confidential."

"Do you believe rapists should be put in prison?"

He answers authoritatively. "I'm speaking from some firsthand knowledge of the California institutions where there's a program of observation for rapists from the date of sentencing until they're placed in a penal institution. If rapists could be placed in a therapeutic hospital program or something like that, where you could get it out, it would help, 'cause so many guys suppress it. When you come here you do time, and that's it. They warehouse people. And when you leave here it's gonna happen again. But I try to be up front with myself, because that's the only person here to be up front with. Nobody else is interested."

Sally changes the subject. "What if you were confronted with one of your victims again?"

Quentin hunches attentively forward in his seat. "It would depend totally on them," he says. "That's exactly it—their reaction to me. I would have to react to their reactions. If it was a screaming, yelling situation, I'd probably first of all let them know, like, 'Well, I've been in a penitentiary, and that's my debt. And if you don't have enough on the gourd to understand that, then I don't think I have to sit here and listen to you.' Just try to put it on them, to let them know that I've paid the cost to society, if that's what society's idea was.

"I've written letters to the girl I raped, and there's no problems in her life. She's happily married. If she ever confronts that situation again, I hope she'll know what to do now. I even gave her some suggestions."

"What kind of suggestions?"

"Not to resist. To play it by ear so she don't get hurt."

"What's your general attitude towards women?" Sally asks.

He thinks for a moment before replying. "For so many years it was a necessity to have one. I've always had a half a dozen close relationships with females, and generally it was always the most beautiful thing I could find on campus or wherever it might have been. But now there will be a lot of curtailing of the four-hundred-a-year type thing—you know, the in and out of bed with everybody. I think a relationship will probably have a hell of a lot more meaning in it now. And more so in what can you do besides screw a chick—that kind of thing."

I ask Quentin about prison gang rapes.

He says that they frequently occur. "If you're effeminate-looking, a little small or weak-looking, this place is hell. If you're not two hundred pounds and lift iron, if you don't stab somebody the first week you're here, there's something definitely gonna happen to you. There's no doubt about it."

Sally wants to know if rapists are especially singled out to be raped by other inmates.

"It depends on what happened in your crime itself," Quentin replies. "If it's a situation where there's somebody here that was related to the victim or knows the people or something like that, you're subject to get raped. There's no doubt about it. Generally in the prison population we're set out. They don't come to you in friendship, you're not invited in the cliques. You have to prove yourself in so many different ways to get into the mainstream of the inmate thing down here. You can be subject to a gang rape if you're a rapist. The thing is, it's usually the guys who at one time or another have raped somebody themselves but are here on another charge—they're usually the ones that come up front and confront you with it."

"The two times you raped, do you think it was out of a feeling of sexual inadequacy?" I ask.

He stares intently at me. "At one time, sure. In respect to the period of time I was being raised by my mother, there was a lot of suppression about masturbation due to the fact that we had an extremely heavy background in the Protestant church. It was frowned upon. For instance, if you jacked off you're going to hell. I was confronted with that so many times that the few times as a child that I did masturbate I was looking for death—a car to run over me, that type of thing. I'm sure it had an effect somewhere. When I got to the point where I could talk a girl into going to bed, it built this macho idea. I had to be the best just from an inadequacy thing, to prove to myself that I wasn't."

"Is there anything you'd like to add?"

He laughs. "I've dreamed so many times of speaking to thousands of women. I'd talk about the porno industry that seems to have brought a lot of moral change about. There's so much freedom involved, and there's a sexual revolution. There might be less rapes going on because of the easiness of having sex with a woman.

"But at the same time, the guys who have been the nice dudes all their life, that all this exposure might bring them out of the closet. That's the fear I have. Where if they can't have that kind of easy relationship with a woman, this is going to make a rapist out of them. You can't characterize. You really don't know. It could be the one you least expect."

141

Part III

THE ILLINOIS PRISONS

Sheridan Correctional Facility

It takes less than an hour from Chicago to reach the Sheridan Correctional Facility in Sheridan, Illinois. Hang a right off the busy expressway that leads to St. Louis, a left at an old country gas station that boasts in crumbly letters "FOOD," and then it's a straight ten-mile stretch to the prison with nothing for company but corn growing high and clear Midwestern sky.

Just before the prison, a road sign announces the town of Norway. It's a tiny, historic hamlet founded in Indian days by Norwegian immigrants who had some grand notions about their settlement's future prosperity. Today, however, Norway isn't even a dot on the state map. It's a quick stopover for visitors to the prison, its only roadside attraction a touristy-looking trading post that sells candy and other gift items.

A few minutes out of Norway, past more empty fields, the Sheridan facility appears unexpectedly—a wired fortress that seems alien in this pastoral setting. It is a modern-looking place, with neat rows of barracks for the prisoners, a large athletic field, and rolling lawns that are cared for by convict trustees. Sheridan is a minimum-security prison—definitely not the kind of joint that Cagney was always trying to break out of.

We enter the long, narrow administrative building, which displays the air-conditioned impersonality of any state-operated agency. Off the hallway correction officials are busily at work in their cubbyholes. The hallway walls are lined with a variety of notices and announcements, and one wall sports Polaroid pictures of convicts at work and play.

A secretary ushers us into the spacious, comfortably furnished office of Warden Dennis Wolff. One wall is covered by a large chart listing the name and offense of every convict serving time at the facility. Wolff is brisk and to the point. He picks up the phone and calls across the yard to have the first prisoner brought over.

"He'll be right here," Wolff says. "How much time will you need with him?"

THE RAPIST FILE

"No more than an hour," I answer. He nods and leads us to a pleasant, pastel-colored interview room. Large bay windows overlook the prison complex. There are no bars on the windows.

"Let me know when you want the next one brought over," Wolff says, and leaves the room.

"The bitches are the type that need to be raped. They need to have it stuffed to them hard and heavy to straighten them out."

Bob enters the interview room like a job applicant trying to make a good first impression. A nervous grin creases his face, and he drawls a thick Dixie "How-do" in greeting. A heavyset Alabaman, he wears Levis and a faded blue workshirt. He sits down at the head of the long table and fumbles with a pack of Winstons. At first he speaks softly and answers questions with a polite "Yes, sir" or "No, sir," but as he begins to relax, his answers become more elaborate.

I ask him a few routine questions about his background, and he replies that he was born in Chicago, moved South with his family, and returned to Chicago several years ago to take a job in the construction industry. Bob says that everything was going fine for him until he was arrested for raping the wife of the man who had hired him. He lights a cigarette, takes a long drag on it, and fiddles with the book of matches.

"Why don't you tell me how it happened," I say.

He shrugs and takes another pull on his cigarette. "It was just going to be a burglary, and there was a person in there, the lady . . . the victim. One thing led to another. I had a hunting knife. I told her to undress and what have you. She did so with no problem. Then the rape took place."

"What about the knife? Would you have used it?"

He nods. "It's like I said. I had this hunting knife, and I imagine if she struggled I would've used it. But she didn't struggle whatsoever. If she had yelled or screamed, that would have probably sent me off the deep end. I might have seriously cut her. You know, down in Alabama I learned to sharpen a knife real good. It was sharp enough so that you could shave with it, so it would have just took the slightest touch in the arm or whatever portion of the body I touched it to, and it would have been laid open." He gestures, as if handling an imaginary knife.

"Did the woman say anything?"

"This lady, she just said, 'Don't hurt me, don't hurt me.' I just told her that if she didn't fight or struggle or anything, she wouldn't get hurt. If she told the police . . . if she didn't tell anybody, she wouldn't get hurt. She told somebody anyhow, and that's why I'm here." He grins incongruously and lights another cigarette.

"Why did you do it?" I ask.

"I don't really know what made me rape her," he says, avoiding my eyes. "It was really weird. I didn't have no problem in getting women, you know. I worked in a nightclub . . . entertainment. I always had women all around."

"Then why?"

He hunches his shoulders and shakes his head. "It was just a thought, something I've never done before. I said, 'Well, I'm going to try this. It's probably nothing I'll ever do again, but I'm not sure.' But, you know—like, I'm young. I don't have no problem in getting women."

"What were you thinking when you were raping her?"

He stares out the window. "It's been quite awhile back, but I remember just thinking about, 'Well, what's going to happen when I get caught—if I get caught?' Because I heard this stuff about long

148

years in prison. I said, 'Well, if I get caught, I'm just going to have to pay the consequences.' It was pretty good. It was stimulating. In a manner of speaking I'll have to admit that. Of course, she was an old lady, I think about sixty-three.

"I didn't really find anything attractive about her—just that she was old and what have you. She probably hadn't had it in a long time. Maybe that's why she didn't put up no fight or struggle—because it was something, maybe part of her youth coming back to her, part of her younger days. And I don't think I wanted to rape her a second time, because the thrill was gone. It was just there for that time, and then it was gone."

"What about afterwards? How did you feel about it?"

Bob smoothes back his hair and shifts in his seat. "I didn't feel that I was normal as a result of raping a woman of that age, doing something like that. I said, 'Man, I've got to be sick.' I talked to a psychiatrist, and it helped me get it together. I'm in a lot better shape than when I first come in. Still, that's something that's part of my past, and I sort of keep it on the inside. When these fellas around here ask me about it, I don't want to talk about it. I figure that it's none of their business. It's still difficult due to the fact of the offense of raping a woman. More the fact that it was an elderly woman. Do you understand? They say, 'Man, this guy is sick.' Here I thought I was too—what time is it, and my life going all right and everything. Two or three different women a day, and then I go out and rape an old woman . . . and get *caught*." He shakes his head in disgust.

"I don't know. Maybe in fifty years, most likely, I'll be able to get it together and run it down—explain what the thrill was. More than anything else, it was probably just getting my nuts off. That had to be—that, right there, had to be—one of the worst wads that I ever shot. One thing about it"—he laughs loudly—"I know that she can't get pregnant. She's too old, so I ain't got that to worry about. I don't know what happened to me. I don't think it will ever happen again, but if it does, it'll probably be with a younger girl, somebody that will have a little bit more body movement and not just lay there like a dead person."

"What are your feelings about women, especially women who get raped?"

"You know, women in general are all right. Some of them is kind, considerate. Some of them is bitches, you know? The bitches are the type that need to be raped. They need to have it stuffed to

149

them hard and heavy to straighten them out." His voice rises. "I mean, these are the women that are up on a high horse, okay? They're stuck up. They think they're better than you. They don't think you're worth throwing their legs up for. So these are the type of women that you have to take it from just to knock them down off that high horse.

"This type of woman ain't nothin'. If she was, she'd give it up, but she ain't nothin'! If she was, she'd be out there on the street throwing her legs up every night, making money at it. But you'll find in normal women that some of them will be reluctant about going to bed with somebody or crawling in the back seat of a car, going out in the bushes or what have you. They'll be reluctant about doing that. But you can usually seduce them, and they'll do it willingly. Then again, there are those hardheads who want to do everything their way. They don't want no part of it, so you have to take it." His face is flushed.

"Are you saying that some women deserve to be raped?" Sally asks.

"I think there are times when rape is . . . relevant. That's a good word. It's kind of big, but it's a good word. There are times when rape is relevant to the circumstances. Then there are times when it's irrelevant. I'm pretty sure of it. I can't seem to get it together enough to say why, because that's something I've never been able to figure out. But maybe someday I'll come up with a solution to it—I done it because of this or because of that or what have you.

"Women also ask for it by these mini-micro skirts, these miniskirts, these hotpants and what have you. And them halter tops! Now, they're just displaying their body. They're saying, 'Hey!' Whether they realize it or not, they're saying, 'Hey, I've got a beautiful body, and it's yours if you want it.' Then, when you take it from them, what do they do? They scream rape.

"I think if a law was passed, there should be a dress code. Then I think rape would stop if they'd make a woman dress decent. When they start dressing in those short skirts and things like that, they're asking for it. When I get married, I'm not going to have my wife going out and wearing short dresses. I'm not going to have her go around with her tits flopping all over the place. I don't want to come home from work some day and find the police standing there and see her on the couch crying, 'Hey, I've been raped.' But whatever the hand calls for, that's what the person is going to get." He

150

breaks off, seeming to fall into a moody reverie.

"How are rapists treated here?" I ask.

"Oh, you're not treated any differently. Not unless you get one of those weird officers—perverts, you know—that's going to say, 'Hey, this guy's here for rape. We're goin' to make it hard on him.' The inmates don't crack about me too often either. I told them, 'Hey, keep your mouth shut about my personal affairs, because I don't go for it.' I don't jump into their personal business, their charge, and I don't want them to come to me with that.

"You know, I write to these various women, and they're turned on by it. Lots of them write back. I don't know whether it's the thought of rape or what it is, but it does something to them. They think about it most likely and say, 'Hey, this is all right. Maybe he'll do it to me.' "

"How would you advise women to react if they're about to be raped?"

"First of all, any woman that goes out and asks for it is going to get it. It's all in the way a person conducts theirself. If they conduct theirself as a lady, clean-cut and what have you, they don't have to worry about any of this. If they conduct theirself as a hussy, then they got it coming by the law of the rapist—get anybody that's asking for it.

"If a decent woman is being attacked, I would advise that the woman not resist, because most rapists, they don't want to inflict pain on the person. They're just in for one thing—to get their nuts off. If the woman doesn't resist, then the chances are high she's not going to get hurt. The only thing that's going to happen is she's just going to get raped and her feelings are going to be upset—her nerves. But if she resists, she's liable to get seriously injured, maybe even killed."

"How many more years are you in for?" I ask, not expecting the answer I get.

Bob grins broadly. "I'll be out in nine months."

Harold, age 30, received a ten-to-thirty-five-year sentence for rape and deviate sexual assault. He served thirteen years of that sentence at the Sheridan Correctional Facility. Harold went before the parole board five times before receiving a parole on October 26, 1978.

I was always scared of people

"She was showing a lot of fear, and that was the thing I was looking for was the fear in her eyes. . . . The women I raped—it seemed like you're a big shot finally, or they're sure the hell scared of you."

"The first one I remember," Harold says, frowning in concentration, "was when I was eight or nine—right around there. It was a party at our house, and there was a little girl, and she was sleeping on the bed. I took off her panties to look at her, and I got caught. Nothing happened when they caught me with that little girl. I was talked to—'This is wrong, that's wrong.' And that was my first experience.

"When I was in military school I was introduced to sex with homosexual practices. I had a cousin, a male cousin, that I con-

153

tinued the practices with when I was at home. Then one time there was a girl downstairs—I was maybe not even ten yet—and I was babysitting for her while her mother and father were out. I exposed myself to her at the time, and when her parents came home the girl mentioned she saw my wee-wee or something like that. Her parents came upstairs and started yelling and screaming at me, and then my mother was the one that always stopped it. 'Don't scream and holler so,' she said. 'Take him out to the amusement park.' So I guess I was kind of rewarded instead of punished." He sighs. "It was right around that time where I started making obscene telephone calls."

Harold is a morose, stocky man with deep-set, brooding eyes. As a result of his behavior, he was placed in a psychiatric hospital at age eleven. While under observation, he continued to make obscene calls from a pay phone.

"When they put me in the psychiatric ward, I was three hundred and twenty pounds. I was always heavy when I was younger, and I was a momma's boy. My people always had money—I guess what you would call upper-middle-class. And when I got out of the hospital, the reward—I guess for losing a lot of weight—was they got me a car. I had a car about every six months after that."

Harold spent four years under psychiatric care. When he was seventeen, he married and had a child. A year later he committed his first rape.

"It started off to me as just a lark. At the time I didn't think I was going out there just to rape a woman. But I wasn't getting along at the house or anything. I didn't have anything to do. I went over to a five-and-dime store near my house and bought a toy pistol. I got one that looked like the real thing, and I was cruising around in the car." He smoothes his hair, which is long and greased back.

"There was a woman walking with a kid in her arms, and I stopped the car and showed her the pistol and asked her if that was her kid. She says yes, and I said, 'If you don't want the kid hurt, throw your purse in the car.' So she threw the purse in the car, and I backed up, and she started walking the other way. I started going down the other way." He frowns.

"Anyhow, I just turned around and pulled into an alley. She was about thirty yards from the car, and I opened up the door and showed her the gun again, and I yelled to her to come on into the car. She started walking away, and I said, 'If you move I'm going to kill you.' She came to the car. I told her to put the kid in the back seat. And she got in the car and everything, and I started driving right around through the alleys, through the streets.

"And I was talking, and I was asking about her sex life and everything, and I asked her when was the last time she was screwed. And she told me, she said, 'The last time I was fucked was last night.' I hit her for that. She said, 'Why did you hit me? I thought that was the way you wanted me to talk.' I told her it wasn't the way I wanted her to talk. After that I told her I wanted her to perform oral sex on me. She said no. I pointed the gun at the back seat at the kid, and she did it. And I tore her blouse and her bra, and I tore her underpants off, and I raped her."

"But the kid—how could you do that with him in the back?" I ask.

He shrugs. "The kid, it didn't bother me at all. I didn't think about him at the time as being there unless she said she wouldn't do something."

"Why this particular woman?"

"It wasn't that I just picked her, it was just that she was the person around. I don't believe I was looking for any type of—you know, any color hair or anything like that she was built in a special way. She was just the one that was there when I was cruising. Prior to that I tried to do the same thing to another woman walking, but she started yelling and screaming and started running. So I just took off. And the next thing, that same evening, this lady was walking down the street nearby. I was eighteen when I did it. She was about thirty-nine."

"If this woman had screamed too, would that have stopped you from raping her?" Sally wants to know.

He nods. "You know, when I brandished the gun to that lady and threatened her and everything, there was a lot of fear. She was showing a lot of fear, and that was the thing I was looking for was the fear in her eyes. And that is what really the thing was all about—that I could instill this fear into her, like when I made the phone calls. I would instill fear to have the people answer my questions by saying I had their husband here. Unless they did what I said, I'd kill him. And it was always on a fear—that I was trying to instill fear into the people. When I did this . . . well, then I attained my goal.

"If the woman hadn't shown fear, I think if she would have just turned around and given me a crack on the head or just said,

'What the hell is wrong with you?' or just started walking away, that was it. Because I don't use violence except the one time I hit her, and I don't even really know why I did that. It just came. It wasn't something that I was mad or anything. It just happened."

"Why did you need to instill fear?" Sally pursues.

"Before the first rape occurred, I was always thinking, 'Why the hell do I have to always come out with money to go?' Like I'd always have a brand-new car, buy this, buy that. I was a good Joe, and I knew why—because I was heavy and everything, and I guess I didn't, wasn't able to, mix with people at all. If I couldn't go somewhere and be the first one there, like the movies—I couldn't stand walking in front of people or anything like that. I had to be either the first one there or the last one so I got the back seat. I wouldn't just come in the middle and say, 'Excuse me' and all that. I just couldn't do it." He looks at me, and his eyes seem to plead for sympathy.

"And I knew I had a sex problem, but the thing was how to relate it to my people and have them—instead of coming out with money all the time—say, 'What in hell . . . ?' That's the way I felt. I was always scared of people. And the women I raped—it seemed like you're a big shot finally, or they're sure the hell scared of you. And a lot of that went through my mind. But what could happen—that didn't even faze me about what could happen until after. Then I heard the police were looking for a car like mine."

"What was your reaction after the first rape?"

A trace of a smile crosses his face. "The strange part about it was, after I dropped her off and threw her purse out the window, is that the next thing I knew I was at my house, and I didn't remember driving home or nothing. It was just like something . . . like I was in a dream and I was coming in my driveway. I knew what had happened. I knew what I had done, but it just didn't dawn on me.

"Like when I was arrested. I was sent to the penitentiary. The psychiatrist—I kept trying to, well, convince him that she wanted to be raped, because I had it in my head that this person just wanted to be raped. I refused to say, 'Well, yeah, I did it.' And I went through a lot of therapy in there and everything else. But from that time after, it was just like I was on a high, but I wasn't high because I didn't take any type of narcotics, I didn't drink. But I was there and I wasn't there. I was looking down on everything, and it just didn't make sense, because I committed two rapes."

"Tell me about the second one," I say.

156

"She was a virgin, and I had her do oral sex to me. How I got her was that I had an envelope in my hand, and I asked her where the address was. And after I started thinking about what happened the first time, I said, 'Damn, it wasn't hard. I got a piece of ass, I got some money too and everything. I'll just do it again.'

"She came to the car and did the same thing. She got in the back seat, and I told her to take her clothes off, and I put my hands between her legs. She was a virgin and started bleeding, and I guess I became more scared than she was. And I told her to get in the front seat, and I had her perform oral sex, and I told her to get out of the car. It bothered me that she was a virgin at the time. I didn't hurt her—just when she started bleeding."

He pauses, lighting a cigarette and blowing a smoke ring. "You know, this was a nineteen-year-old, and the thing about it, she was just about built the same. They were both, not heavy, but kind of chunky. And I guess—well, I don't know if they were. I can't remember if they looked the same or not.

"Anyway, later I was going to pick up my girl because I was hungry." He chuckles at the recollection. "So food was my downfall, I guess, because I stopped at a hamburger joint, and the cops—I didn't notice them when I pulled out of my driveway about two blocks away. And I came out, and the next thing I knew there were squad cars there, detectives there, pistols, rifles and everything, and they had them pointed at me. They asked the younger one if this was the person that did it, and she said yes. They brought me to the police station and had a lineup and everything. And I was convicted on the two crimes that I did do."

Sally picks up the questioning. "Do you think women ask to be raped?"

"I don't think that I believe women go out there and look for rape. Sure, some of them may wear miniskirts and nothing underneath their clothes—but I don't wear shorts sometimes." He grins. "You know, I guess if I was a chick and I had good legs and I wanted to wear a miniskirt, that's what I would wear. I don't believe that because a girl is walking around the streets and she's showing a little bit that she wants somebody to pick her up and go ahead and do something to her. This is just clothes. I think a rapist that does it puts in his mind that the clothes is why he did it. Otherwise he's not going to be able to do it."

"How should women act if they're in danger of being raped?"

"I think that if a chick is approached by anybody—I know

157

about me—that instead of just acting scared, do the opposite. If I was a girl I'd stand up to him and say, 'What the hell is your problem?'—start yelling and run. Of course, I believe that if a woman were to start screaming or yelling, that seventy-five percent of the rape would never happen—unless it's a guy that's drunk, on dope or anything. He's not just looking for rape, he's looking for money and stuff too. And if he's high or if he's drunk or anything, you know, he's not together himself anyhow too much. He's going to try to stop the girl from screaming. But I know that if the people were to scream at me in both cases, I don't think I'd be here.

"I don't believe that what they're saying in the papers and on TV is what's really happening out there. Like we've got the cops telling women don't fight. Now, that's ridiculous, because if a woman doesn't fight, that's exactly what a guy's looking for. He's looking for a passive chick. Like I said," he repeats with feeling, "for me, if the girl just would have—if this one chick in the car would have slapped my face and started calling me names and saying, 'What would your mother think of you?' and this and that, I probably would have driven her home, apologized. That's what I believe. I believe that passive is crap unless someone's got a knife up to their throat. But then I believe that a person can talk themselves out of it or run or something. But I don't believe that a woman should just take a passive role."

"When do you think you'll get out of prison?" I ask.

"I don't have any idea when I'll be out of here. Like I've gone through everything they've got here. I've got my high school equivalency, I've gotten four years of college, and I've just about been in every vocational program. I've had about two or three years of therapy—individual therapy—seeing a psychiatrist here on a voluntary basis every couple of months. The last time, I really thought I'd make parole," he says despondently.

"Has therapy helped you?"

"What it's done is it made me grow up. It's made me be able to think about what happened and get it out of my mind that she wanted to be raped. Like if you would have asked me that question six, seven, or eight years ago, I would say, 'Yeah, sure, she wanted to be raped. She was walking around with no stockings on. She wanted to be raped.' But that's not in my head now."

"Then why do you think they've kept you here so long?"

"I guess the parole board is still under the impression that I'm still kind of oversexed, because when I went to the board the last

158

time, they looked up what happened when I was almost ten years old, and they said, 'Damn, you've been oversexed since you've been nine years old.' You can't answer them. I told the guy, I said, 'Maybe you think I'm oversexed, but you're wrong. I don't know where you're coming from.' This is a problem I keep having with them. They keep looking at my records when I was nine or ten years old. They refuse to look at my stuff now. I say, 'If you think I'm the same person that I was at nine and a half, you better get the hell out of this office, because you shouldn't be on the board.'

"Rape is considered more serious than murder because I guess murder is something that happens once. But no one can ever tell if a guy who's here for rape is going to walk out in the streets and do it again. There's just one way you can tell a guy—by turning him loose and see what happens. I think that basically that's what they're afraid of."

"Are you sure you wouldn't rape again?"

He frowns and lights another cigarette. "I don't have any feelings about me going out and jumping off a tree, or when you look at a chick and say, 'Any way I can, I'm going to get her.' Before, when I saw a female, I'd get uptight and nervous. I couldn't talk, hands are sweating, my tongue would get dry. I'd say, 'Damn, I've got to figure out a way to get her.' And it just doesn't act that way now, and I guess I can take it or leave it as it comes. If it comes, it comes. If it doesn't, it doesn't. Like I've got a chick out there now. I don't know how long she's going to wait. But I just believe now that if I can get paroled, I'm ready for it."

The interview time is almost up, and I am just about to turn off the tape recorder when Harold says, "Do you want to know another reason why I would never rape again? I'll tell you why. There's two more good reasons. I was eighteen years old chronologically when I entered prison, but emotionally I'd say I was about ten. I just wasn't allowed to grow up. Now I'm thirty years old, so there's been a lot of growing up to do—a lot of wasted years for nothing, you know? And I've just got too many things outside to do to be coming back to the penitentiary for anything."

"What's the other reason?"

"I wouldn't want to rape again because I know how it feels. When I was in the county jail I was raped by twelve guys. They busted my head, and I was unconscious. I know how it feels. . . ."

159

Menard Correctional Center

Chester, Illinois, is a sleepy Mississippi River town that recently gained a spectacular sort of notoriety when a UFO magazine published a cover story claiming that the town was totally devastated by an invasion of flying saucers. Residents reacted to all the hoopla with calm bemusement, assuring the hordes of reporters who flocked to the town that life remained essentially the same as it had been since the early French settlers first arrived.

Aside from this brief flirtation with national prominence, about the only thing that distinguishes Chester—located approximately one hundred miles southeast of St. Louis—from the dozens of other towns that hug the Mississippi is the presence here of one of the state's largest maximum-security institutions, Menard Correctional Center.

The locals are as indifferent to the penitentiary's location in Chester as they were to reports that their town had been wiped out by alien invaders. But to a visitor viewing for the first time this massive prison complex with its towering smokestack, it has a sinister air. Built in the 1800s, it is the oldest prison in the state, and age has left its oppressive scrawl everywhere.

Menard is set in the foot of a valley at the end of a narrow road that winds along the banks of the Mississippi past stately river homes that have long since seen better days. Ordinarily it's a pretty drive, but this afternoon even the proximity of the mighty Mississippi brings no relief from the sweltering heat. The penitentiary looms suddenly ahead, and we gratefully pull into the visitors' parking lot, relieved to be out of the car.

In the "roundhouse"—the visitors' entry point—two prison guards warily check our credentials and ask us to deposit into a locker money, cigarettes, and whatever other personal possessions we may be carrying. The guards will not allow Sally to enter the main structure. They carefully frisk me before escorting me across a small courtyard through two massive steel gates.

On the inside, a sense of anxiety suddenly sweeps over me as I

161

realize that I'm locked in a prison with some of the toughest cons the state has to offer. I breathe an inaudible sigh of relief as a prison supervisor arrives and guides me to a small room to wait for the first of the rapists I'll be interviewing this afternoon.

Phil, age 42, was given a fifteen-to-twenty-year sentence on five counts of rape, kidnapping and aggravated assault. He served nine years of that sentence at Menard Correctional Center and is presently out on parole.

"It's not like stealing someone's property.
If you've raped a woman, you can't undo that.
One of the girls said to me, 'Why me?'
The only answer I can give to that is that you
happened to be in the wrong place at the
right time."

Phil is a lanky, nervous type with Ben Franklin glasses and the demeanor of a Rhodes scholar. He has an intellectual bent and tends to analyze everything he says almost to the point of distraction. He has obviously read voluminously on the subject of rape.

Phil continually punctuates his conversation with references to source material I've never heard of. Within ten minutes of our first meeting, he produces a half-finished manuscript about rape and a boxful of poems that he wants me to have published. I steer the conversation back to its original purpose.

163

"Tell me something about yourself."

"I'm forty-two years old, and I've been an electronics engineer since 1965," he says. "I was married in 1957, and I have a daughter. I was employed by the Boeing Company until 1969 at Huntsville, Alabama, at which time I came up to Chicago to take over my father's business. My wife stayed down there. About a year after taking over my father's business, I went out and raped five times."

"What made you rape?" I ask.

He laughs. "Oh, a whole lifetime. It's just living, really. It's not easy—that's why it's taken so long to think it all out. From what I've gotten out of my analysis, a lot of things have emerged. How pivotal this is depends on how you approach it, I suppose. I was raped myself when I was nine years old. I never told Mother about it. It left me with very strong feelings of shame and guilt and difficulty in relating to women. Instead of trying to seek any relationships with them in the real world, I would retreat into my fantasies. Even at the earliest stage I can remember doing that.

"The primary problem, as I see it, is a failure to ever learn to love and how to love. That stemmed from a blocked love relationship with my mother at a very early age. It wasn't that my mother didn't love me; Mother never knew how to express the love to me. She was just never able to do it." He speaks about his mother very softly, and his voice trails off at the end of each sentence.

"So I grew up with tremendous feelings of inferiority in this area, tremendous feelings of not being able to relate to women. Of course, when I reached puberty I was sexually attracted to them. But it was a thing where I was attracted to them and there was fear at the same time. I knew a number of girls when I was young, but I never had any satisfactory relationship with any girls. They all turned sour, every single one of them. . . . Never had a satisfactory sexual relationship. In fact, I never had a sexual relationship until I was married—and then it wasn't satisfactory. It never has been.

"I might say that to this day I've never had a loving sexual relationship with any woman. Looking back at my life, I can see a number of elements running through it because of this blocked relationship with my mother. I grew up continually seeking love from a woman but always not being able to relate to them in a manner which would allow them to reciprocate. So I just began to retreat more and more within myself and my own fantasy world."

His voice grows stronger as he continues. "But I went on and

164

did what my parents wanted me to do—become an engineer, which wasn't what I wanted to do. I wanted to become a musician. I had studied piano and music all my life. The Korean War was facing me, and I was going to be drafted. I didn't know what to do, because I couldn't get a deferment because of music college.

"At that time I had a very strong relationship going with a girl. She was seventeen and I was nineteen. Catherine. I guess you'd call it puppy love at that age, but there were strong, true feelings there. But we're both Catholics, and we both drove ourselves nuts wanting to have a sexual relationship and couldn't bring ourselves to do it. The affair broke off when I went into the service, leaving us both feeling very sour and very guilty over the whole thing. And that state of affairs persisted until I had my therapeutic breakthrough. After that I met a number of other girls, but for one reason or another they all rejected me. So I suffered tremendous feelings of rejection at that moment." He pauses briefly.

"When I was overseas in England I met my wife. She was running away. She was about to get married at one time, and her father had put the halt on everything. Her fiancé shows up in the evening the day before they're going to get married, and he says, 'My mother says you've got to give this up and you have to give up that.' So she took the ring, and her father even kicked him out the door. Which was a good thing to do, because her fiancé made her feel really bad. So she falls in love with this Norman guy, and Norman one day comes over and says, 'I'm sorry, I can't love you. I'm a homosexual.' It shattered her, and she hasn't been able to love since. On the rebound two weeks later she meets me, so as an escape she comes to the States with me when I get out of the service.

"One of the feelings I now had to face was that I married my wife at that time purely out of feelings of sex. There was no real love feelings there at the time. I actually was rather pushed into the marriage by some friends of ours who thought it was a good idea. And we were too stupid to realize that we should have given it a chance, wait six months or so and see what our real feelings were. But she wanted to escape, and I was looking for sex." He sighs.

"So we got married and came back to the States, and that's when the troubles started with the marriage. My mother disapproved of her, and I was really attached to my mother, because as I said, my mother wasn't able to give me love, and I was continually seeking it from her—couldn't break loose of Mother. Of course, my wife had accused me of it many times, but I denied it.

"So I got back to the States and decided to get a degree in engineering—going to school nights, working during the days. Then my wife and I took an apartment at my parents' place, and right from the start my wife and mother took a dislike to each other. Nothing but battles, arguments, back and forth. And I sided with my mother against my wife—'You're the one with psychological problems, you're not adjusting,' this and that.

"Well"—he sighs again—"my wife began to come apart. She had a crack-up. I took her to the hospital, and she went through some therapy, and she finally quit it. Finally things came to a head in '59. I had a chance to take a contract to do some field engineering, and she decided—well, actually it was mutual agreement—to go back to England. But what she did, she went back to a bad environment with her parents. And so she cracked up over there again and had further psychiatric treatment.

"She came back to the States finally when I'd finished the contract. By that time my parents had moved out to Westchester, and I was living with them, working for my father during the day in his business. My dad wanted me to take over the business all his life, and I didn't want it—that was a continuous source of friction between us. And I was going to school nights getting my engineering degree. When my wife came back, my folks offered to let us live there. They had plenty of room, and we'd save expenses if we did that. Of course, our daughter had been born at that time, and my wife put her in school.

"During that time my wife was taking care of the house, and of course my mother began to dictate to her—'Do this and do that since you're at home.' That really degenerated into a bad situation, and my wife started drinking and taking pills and threatened suicide. She did try to commit suicide twice, I believe. So I took her down to the hospital, and she started psychological counseling there which she stuck with for about six or seven months, and then she gave it up.

"So things were at an impasse, they were really bad. It was at this point that I really began to come apart, with all the pressures on me at work, this blocked relationship with my mother and my wife, trying to get that degree. I was working during the day, come home at four-thirty, eat, and at five-thirty leave for school, come home at night and study until two-thirty in the morning. My wife was drunk half the time, couldn't cope, couldn't face anything, and

I was too stupid to realize what was going on. I needed to get her out of there. Finally I did get my degree and took the job at Boeing Aerospace Division in Huntsville, Alabama. We bought a home down there, and things were pretty good for awhile. Of course, this was at the peak of the aerospace industry in '65, but it was downhill after that. The job began to come apart, and my sense of security began to fall apart."

"When did you commit the first rape?"

"Let me back up a little bit. While we were still living up in Westchester and my wife was drinking so heavily, she tried to commit suicide by taking an overdose. When I came home one night my mother said, 'You better go see about your wife. I think she just killed herself.' So I went in the bedroom, and she was just barely conscious, and she says she took a whole bottle of sleeping pills and she was going to die. I knew there was only a half a bottle because I had looked at it that morning. So I sat with her the rest of the night, and she came out of it finally. I was going to call the hospital, but my mother said, 'No, I don't want any police here.' So I listened to my mother all the way on this thing." Another sigh.

"But it wasn't long after that. You see, all my life I'd had trouble with trying to act out a lot of these sexual conflicts. At first they'd be fantasies in my mind, and then maybe they'd come out later in behavior like running around in the streets naked at night when I was a little kid—never much farther than around the house." Again he sighs loudly. "Terrific feelings of guilt over masturbation. Of course, being a Catholic, you know how they are about that. I thought the whole vengeance of God was going to come down on me.

"So this behavior started up again about that time, when I was having all this trouble with my wife—and I found myself wandering around the streets naked at night looking in homes for a naked woman. And then I started breaking in homes. There was one woman in the neighborhood, I broke in with the intent of raping her, and I got all the way over to the bed and pulled the sheet back, and she was lying there naked. I panicked and ran away. I went back to the same woman again, only this time she woke up as I was leaving and knew someone was in the house, and she called the police. That was about six months apart.

"Then that situation finally degenerated, and one night I was coming home from school feeling really depressed. I had been drinking a lot—the drinking thing, you use that as a justification for

167

a thing you know you're going to do all along anyway." He pauses to let his point sink in. "So I started roaming the streets in the old neighborhood where I used to live in Cicero, and I found a girl walking the streets, and I attacked her. She screamed and I ran off. That happened again about six months later, the same way.

"So then nothing further happened until we moved to Huntsville and the job began to fall apart after about the first three and a half or four years. I began to disintegrate, come apart. Our marriage was surprisingly better at that time because we were away from the friction of my parents. But it wasn't better with me as far as my state of mind. And, of course, my dad was really pressuring me to take over the business because he wanted to retire. And Mom being in the business, she took over the front office. They both wanted to get the hell out of it.

"So I started looking around for another job, and everything was shaky. Aerospace bottomed out in '70, but this was '68, and they saw it coming. So I said to my dad one time at Christmas, 'Goddamn, if you still want me to take over the business, make me a definite offer.' So he did, and it was too attractive to turn down. I was looking for security. See, this is one of the things I recently realized. I was looking for the wrong things—I was looking for security over love because I didn't know how to love." He stares at me for emphasis.

"So what happened then, I came up to Chicago, and my folks and I were talking about the business, and I was unpacking in the bedroom. They were in the kitchen. And I suffered some sort of depressive reaction—I just collapsed on the bed and began crying hysterically because I had separated my feelings from my family in Huntsville and put my ass up in Chicago where I didn't belong." Phil reflects for a moment, then resumes. "I didn't realize what that was, though—I just suffered the reaction.

"Well, things went along until Christmastime, when my wife and child came down to spend Christmas with the relatives and everything. I put them on a plane and sent them back and had the same sort of reaction. This was in January of '70. Well, in April my parents took off for Hawaii on a vacation for a whole month and left me to take care of the business and the home by myself. This is when it hit me and I came to find the whole responsibility of the business on my shoulders all of a sudden. The sense of loss I was feeling for not having anyone—I was on my own totally, and I couldn't handle that sense of insecurity. The awareness was just too much.

"So I began driving down streets, and I wasn't really in control of myself at all. My subconscious mind was in control. It was just my needs finally taking over. I don't know how many girls I attempted to pick up at the point of a gun." He lowers his voice. "I looked at that very carefully. There was never any serious intent on my part of ever using that gun. But the fact was that it was loaded, and I could have if I panicked. There was a real danger there, there was no question about it."

"You don't know how many rapes you attempted?" I ask.

"Oh, lord, I lost track. Between twenty and thirty. I was running wild. I'd be coming home in the evening, and all of a sudden I'm not going home, and I'd spend the rest of the evening driving around and maybe attack two or three girls. I only succeeded in picking up five girls. Each time the behavior was the same. I'd pick them up by gunpoint, put them in the car, blindfold them with tape, gag 'em and tie their hands, and I'd take 'em back to the house, to the bedroom which my wife and I had used. I'd act out this whole conflict situation I had with my wife, and this was a surrogate substitute. Of course she didn't respond, and it was just me aggressing on her.

"I didn't hurt any of the girls other than psychologically. But I did some pretty bizarre things—stick Coke bottles up them, and that kind of stuff," he says matter-of-factly. "This is the thing. It was a sexual aggression. But there was no violence on my part. I didn't want to hurt the women—I wanted the women to love me is what it was. But of course it was impossible under those circumstances. But that's the kind of state of mind I was in.

"So this happened five times, and the fifth time I picked up two girls simultaneously and took 'em back to the house and tied 'em down to the bed. I shaved their pubic hair and did all sorts of acting-out behavior. And after the fifth time they finally had enough information on me to pick me up on the basis of the description of the car. I was going out to see a customer in Naperville, Illinois, and I guess they had a bulletin on me. The cops stopped me and arrested me.

"The funny thing about this is the state of mind I was in. I had read about this and seen my picture in the paper—you know, they'd drawn a sketch of me. I wanted to be caught. There's no question about it. I just ignored that and continued to go about my daily affairs, driving around—and I had a bright yellow car, you couldn't miss it." He laughs. "And out-of-state license plates—I mean, really . . ."

169

"Did the sketch in the paper resemble you?"

He laughs again. "Oh, yes. That's what's interesting about the state of mind I was in. Now, if I was in a logical or rational mind, I would say, 'Now I've got to get rid of that car, leave the state, go home, or do something.' But no. I just went about my business. They picked me up because I wanted to be caught. When I was arrested I totally came apart in the jail, and the doc says, 'He's crazy, he's psychotic.' They put me in Cook County Jail and had me in the hospital for a whole year while the case was being adjudicated. They tried to get me down here as a Sexually Dangerous Person, but they never applied that because of the publicity on the case. Finally they decided to give me fifteen to twenty on the rapes and less on the other stuff. They'd all run concurrently, which was a damn big break."

"So how long have you been in?"

"I've been locked up now six years, and I'm going on my seventh year. I go for parole in '79. If I don't make it then, five months later I max out. So I'm pretty close to getting out."

"Do you recall what went through your mind during any of the attacks?"

"Oh, yeah. You see, all these attacks, I fantasized them out ahead of time. I knew exactly what I was going to do. So all I did was relive these fantasies with the girls when I actually did pick them up."

"What did you talk to them about?"

"Very little verbal contact. There was some. There was no attempt to kiss the girls or to relate to them as human beings or as individuals. That's not where I was at. I was using them strictly as a sex object in which to act out all these conflicts and blocked relationships with my wife. Mainly in the sexual area, but not completely. There was a communication problem with my wife. We were never able to communicate. That's the theme that's been running through all of this. I've never been able to effectively communicate until this therapeutic breakthrough. I just couldn't bring myself to do that. I just couldn't talk about it. In fact, my brother-in-law said to me at the time I was arrested—I've got two brother-in-laws, one's an attorney, and the other's a psychiatrist—they said, 'Goddamn, Phil, why the hell didn't you talk to me about this?' I says, 'Well, I couldn't.' And at that time I couldn't."

"You would stop and point a gun at the women you raped?"

"Well, you see, initially I didn't use a gun. I had just tried to

170

grab 'em and pick 'em up. And then later I had some chloroform, and that didn't work. I used a knife one time, but then when they'd scream I'd run away—I couldn't hurt the girls. I had to work that through. The answer to that is no, I wouldn't have. My psychiatrist pointed that out. He said, 'You're not that type of rapist, a rapist-murder type. You're not that type at all.' So I'm relieved at that, because if I had really hurt those girls physically, I couldn't have handled that. I would have killed myself."

"What happened after you raped them?"

"After it was all over, what I would do is take them back to where I picked them up. Now, they saw me when I picked them up, and they saw me when I let 'em off, but in the state of mind I was in that didn't bother me."

"Did the women say anything at this point?"

"Oh"—he sighs—"I think one of the girls one time said, 'Oh, my nylons are torn' or something, and I gave her some money to replace the nylons." He breaks out laughing. "It's very bizarre. It's all in my journal. Like I say, someday I want to put a book together and get it all out."

"Was there any particular type of woman you sought out?" I ask.

"All of these girls were young, in the area of about fifteen to twenty. I was thirty-seven when I was doing all this. A lot of what I was doing I think was not only acting out a conflict with my wife and, of course, with my mother, but with this girl Catherine that I had known at age seventeen. That had been my very first strong relationship with a woman, the most intimate level I've ever reached with a woman. And because that thing had been left unresolved, I think a lot of this acting out that was going on was trying to relive that situation with Catherine. I think that was part of the reason I picked girls in this age bracket, because I used to deliberately look for women in this age category."

"Any special type of looks?"

"Yeah, usually very pretty women—you know, nicely dressed, short skirts. I had a definite image of a female in my mind. A kind of goddess-on-a-pedestal sort of thing. See, it goes back even farther than I can remember, to when I was a kid in grammar school adoring the blessed Virgin Mary thing they used to beat into you. In a way this was also in my mind—to fuck the blessed Virgin Mary. Boy, I remember one girl I was really attracted to, but I was so afraid of women when I was in grammar school that all I could

171

do was idolize her from across the street. When I'd see her coming down the street, I had to turn the other way. I couldn't even walk by her."

"Did any of your victims struggle?"

"No. You see, I was very clever the way I did all this. I said something to the effect that if you do what I ask, you won't be hurt. They were sufficiently intimidated with the gun that they wouldn't struggle or anything. In fact, if there was any struggle on the part of a woman, I would back off right away. I wouldn't persist. I couldn't handle that, because that would be relating with the girl. That's what I couldn't handle. In fact, one of the girls enjoyed it, and she wanted to do it again, and I panicked." He laughs. "She was getting aggressive, and I panicked. So I said, 'No, that's enough,' and I got her dressed and took her in the car and took her back."

"Did the rapes live up to your expectations?"

"Well, it didn't solve anything as far as my conflicts go. I mean, there was a release, of course, of sexual tension for a couple of days, and then it returned. It always culminated in my having intercourse with them. But they were just a passive object. In fact, I had to tie them down to do it. You see, I couldn't allow them to respond at all."

"What were your feelings afterwards?"

"Oh, I would feel shitty with myself for having done that. Tremendous feelings of guilt. But yet, the compulsion to do it again would always return. In my state of mind I would have continued raping until I was caught, which is what happened.

"It was only as a last resort that I used a gun to get what I wanted. The compulsion was so strong that I had to get it. I had strong reservations about using a gun, and then I would only allow myself to point that thing at her. I couldn't cock it, although it was loaded. In fact, there is one girl I did that with, and she just stood there shocked and didn't move. I asked her to get in the car, and when she didn't do anything I just drove away." He laughs. "I couldn't press it any farther than that."

"You say you were glad when you were caught?"

"Oh, definitely. I couldn't go on like that. I would have hurt myself or somebody else."

"So therapy in prison has helped you?"

"Oh, it's definitely helped me."

"Do you feel when you're paroled you may rape again?"

172

"No, I've blown that. In fact, the title of this book I'm writing is titled *Ex-Rapist*. See, what I had to do in this therapy is relive that whole doggone relationship problem with a woman, a significant female. In this case it was my mother. I can now accept trying to relate with a woman and risk rejection. All my life I've had rejection from everyone, and I couldn't handle it. Now I know what I want out of life. I've turned my priorities around, and now I'm seeking love and loving relationships with people. I want only honest relationships with people. No more forcing, no more phoniness, no more fear over having to expose myself and become vulnerable—especially to a woman. That's what I had to do over there, allow myself to become vulnerable and to feel hurt if there was to be hurt. And there was hurt associated with it, and it was difficult to handle it. But I handled it. I went through it."

"What kind of psychological scars do you have as an ex-rapist?" I ask.

"There is residual guilt over what I've done, and through the writing of my book I'd like to set the record straight if I could. In the last section I've got a little thing here which deals with an idea I had which I think might be of some social benefit." He reads from his journal.

One final word. Anyone who has even seen the movie *Death Wish* will recall that the young girl is committed to a mental hospital in a state of catatonia which presumably she will never recover from. This may be an overly severe reaction, but it's not unknown to happen. However, I believe that most women, when they have had a traumatic experience of rape or sexual assault, are bound to have some sort of psychological reaction, and it might well result in a lasting conflict situation that can color and affect the rest of their relationships in life, either with themselves or with others.

There is a case that can be made for a woman to confront her attacker at the time of the arrest. This is to present her a human being of flesh and blood on which she can focus her fears so that they don't remain a nameless fear in her mind forever. I believe that based on my experience, that a good case could be made for confronting a woman with her attacker at any time if she still has a psychological problem as a result of the attack and if she desires it and if her doctor or psychiatrist deems it advisable and for her therapeutic benefit.

But she isn't the only one that I feel could probably benefit from such a meeting. The rapist, if he has worked through his problem and is ready, could also probably benefit by being given the opportunity to tell the woman that he is sorry for what he did.

"I know that I feel that I could possibly benefit from it in that I could at least have the opportunity to offer to say I'm sorry. This could go a long way toward relieving any feelings of guilt that I may still have."

"So you believe the rapist and his victims should meet?"

"Exactly. I'm going to pursue this myself on the other side. I'd at least like to be able to make the offer to these women I raped. I know one that does have sexual problems. I did find that out. Whether she still does today I don't know—after all, it's been six years. But if any of them still have any problems that have affected their relationships and I'm the cause of it, I'd at least like to try to offer to do something about that."

"What exactly are you going to say to these women?"

He answers quietly. "I'm sorry."

"Is that enough?"

He sighs. "I would hope so. I don't know what else one can do. It's not like stealing someone's property. If you've raped a woman you can't undo that. One of the girls said to me, 'Why me?' The only answer I can give to that is that you happened to be in the wrong place at the right time. It's unfortunate."

"Do you think that most women want to be raped?"

"I definitely had that orientation. I felt that women very much wanted to be taken. Today, no. I respect a woman's uniqueness and her individuality, her right to her own body and own mind. There's a point you can go in a relationship with any person, I think, and you have no right to cross beyond that."

"Do you think your punishment fits your crime?"

"At the time I got the conviction I was very angry that they'd given me so much time. But, of course, I couldn't see any other perspective, because compared to what I could have gotten—life on any one of those charges—I can see now they were working very hard to give me every possible break they could. I mean, it was a pretty severe crime I did. Looking back today, no, I'm not angry at the punishment that was imposed.

"But if there is any anger, it is that we're handling this whole problem of rape in a very irrational manner. For instance, this whole question of whether or not I was sane or insane never occurred in the whole adjudication of my trial. They removed that issue entirely because it was too hot, too sensitive. I had a state attorney there that wanted to satisfy the public's cry for vengeance. They had tremendous publicity in the papers about it. Yet, looking back on it, I'm convinced now that I really was flipped out. There's no question in my mind about that. Twenty-one counts of that kind of behavior should speak for itself."

"Twenty-one counts?"

"There were seven indictments. Five rapes, and the rest of them were like aggravated assault, kidnapping—all related to the rape incidents. I feel that if there had been some sort of procedure set up to determine 'Is this person operating in a rational, sane manner?' they would have seen that I was in more need of treatment than punishment. But they chose due to the politics of the situation to punish me and give me treatment later.

"You find this theme running through the whole prison system. Rehabilitation seems to play second fiddle to the question of vengeance. Then, after the punishment, if you're still alive then we'll try and rehabilitate you. But I don't think anybody can rehabilitate you. I think that all that can be done is the opportunity being offered you. I think you've got to rehabilitate yourself. And when I could come to that realization finally through my therapy, I realized that no one else is going to do it for me. And if I don't do it while I'm here, I'm liable to go back out on the street and do the same damn thing again. And that I didn't want."

"Do you feel that most rapists need therapy rather than punishment?" I ask.

"I would say in a large percentage of the cases, yes. It's a psychological problem, a severe psychological problem that demands the best that our scientists are able to bring to bear on the problem. And yet it doesn't. The Department of Corrections has to operate on such a shoestring budget. Things have shifted a little bit now with the federal government putting more money into it. We've got more services and young, dedicated people coming into it, but what they lack is experience that will come with the years, of course."

"What advice would you give women about avoiding rape?"

"That's a difficult thing, because what are you going to tell a woman? 'Hey, don't go outdoors'? I mean, she has just as much right to walk down the street as a man does. But they should be aware that there is this real risk out there on the streets, that there are men in the situation I was in running around on the streets. I think they need to have a more rational concern about themselves and their self-interest. Of course, don't go walking the streets at night alone where there's no lights or things like that. You're asking for trouble when you do things like that."

"Do you think women should carry weapons for self-defense?"

"No, I don't think that's the answer," Phil replies quickly. "We've got too much violence in this country today as it is. If a woman started carrying around a gun, I think she'd run a real risk, because there are some types of rapists that if she aggresses back, they get angry then, and then they're really liable to hurt them.

"But women should just use more common sense. Because I can think when I was driving around and looking, looking, looking, I'd see so many women doing so many stupid things, to my way of thinking. Now, here I was looking for a woman to pick up and rape, and I was empathizing with them—'Gee, you're asking for trouble.' But maybe she wasn't my type or something." He laughs. "They've got to accept the fact that not all men are the kind of men that they'd like them to be. There are lots of messed-up men walking the streets."

Luke, age 28, was charged with rape, attempted murder and armed robbery. He was sentenced to ten to twenty years at Menard Correctional Facility, where he served ten years. He was released on supervision on March 7, 1980.

"It's humiliating, but it's not as bad as the way everybody is thinking. If you're not pregnant, stop and think. It's not all that bad. It'll be in your mind probably, as it'll be in his mind. And he's sick. All you do is let yourself get sick—'I'm a nervous wreck, and I can't mess with men anymore.' That's not cool either. But I don't think it's all that bad."

A young man quietly enters the room. Short and slightly built, he has penetrating eyes that gaze out with catlike intensity.

When he was sixteen years old, Luke was arrested for rape and committed to Menard as a Sexually Dangerous Person—a classification that calls for intensive psychiatric treatment. Because he

177

was so young, he received preferential treatment from the courts. Despite the many rapes he confessed to, he was out on the street four years after he entered Menard. A year after his release, Luke was back behind bars. Again the charge was rape, but this time there was no leniency.

"What made a young guy like you start raping women?" I ask after listening to several minutes' worth of complaints about prison life.

"I was born in Chicago in 1951. I was raised Catholic. My father worked nights, and my mother was suffering from multiple sclerosis. About 1962 I noticed a change in her personality. I was about twelve. She started talkin' more and more to me and not getting along with my old man. She started transferrin' some of this frustration toward me. She was getting on my case and stuff. I was trying to understand what was happening, and then again, I wasn't picking up everything. That is what set me in the streets, started me hangin' out in the streets." His eyes bore into mine.

"How many women did you rape?"

He laughs. "Well, when I got arrested my father came to see me. He was shakin' his head, and he said, 'You know, son, you made the newspapers.' I said, 'Yeah?' He said, 'They got you down for sixty or seventy rapes.' I'll put it like this. One day I sat down and tried to remember, and I came up with twenty-six. It might've been more."

"How many more?"

"I raped for two years. If you want to put it on an average, maybe two or three times a month. It seems to me like every time something didn't go right in the crib, I'd leave and rape someone. It wasn't like no sexual urge that I gotta have some, 'cause I got some all the time"—he laughs again—"with my little ol' girlfriend. It wasn't because I couldn't get sex."

"What kind of women did you rape?"

"The majority of them were between twenty and forty years old. This was on the South Side of Chicago, a black neighborhood called Englewood. In a way it was a thrill for some reason because they were scared. You know—'I gotcha.' They didn't want to do it, and that's what really turned me on. I was makin' them do something they didn't want to do. Then they got to cryin'. If they cried it was just a bigger kick.

"But after I'd do it and I'm runnin' away, I'd get to feelin' bad. I knew I was doin' wrong. There was a couple of times I

178

was goin' to sit down and tell a priest that things just ain't together. I didn't. I just kept doing that." He pauses and fumbles for a cigarette.

"So you liked the power over these women, is that it?" I ask as he lights up.

He nods. "That was my goal. It was to humiliate them. That's what the goals of rapists are—to humiliate. To me it was more like a revenge type of thing. During the rape all I was thinking about was watchin' them. I remember there was one or two women that seemed like they enjoyed it. They might've been faking it and tryin' to keep me from hurtin' them. And I really didn't get as big a thrill out of it. The ones that seemed really frightened is the ones that really turned me on. That's what I'd need, you know?

"I didn't like for them to talk to me either. That seemed to anger me more. But if it seemed that they was scared, that was all right. If they got to 'Baby, why you doin' this?' or 'You don't got to do this'—one woman, I remember, she said, 'If you want some sex, I'm no whore'—it just seemed to get me angrier. I'd threaten them, act like I was goin' to hit them. I very seldom hit them."

"What do you mean by 'very seldom'?"

Luke seems to answer a bit reluctantly. "There were ones I cut. The ones I cut were the ones that fought back physically. I think those are the ones I really didn't do anything to them sexually. They was trying to get away, and they was trying to call for help. One woman actually thought she could overpower me. I didn't stab her. I remember the cut was right on her hand somewhere. The idea of getting caught really didn't excite me."

"How did you get your victims?"

He takes a deep drag on his cigarette before answering. "A majority of times me and my momma would get into it, or she'd start buggin' me in some way and I'd leave. And I carried a knife with me always. And I'd just get to walkin' the streets trying to figure out what was goin' on. I'd see some woman, and I'd get to looking at her. I'd get relatin' her to Mom, you know? Here Ma talked all this shit, and I'd get the urge to fix her. So I'd follow the woman along, and the first dark alley or darkest street they come to with nobody around, what I'd do is go threaten her. I'd grab her and make sure they see the knife. And I told them, 'If you scream I'll kill you.'

"Not all the women I grabbed submitted. Some of them fought back, and I split because I don't think I actually wanted to hurt

179

them physically—cut 'em up like that. I don't think I cut but maybe two or three women, and that's because they tried to wrestle and scream for help—the fear of being caught. They weren't hurt real bad. I had one indictment for assault.

"But they'd usually submit, and I'd get them in an alley behind the house or wherever we may be. I'd make them take off their clothes and rape them. I found the majority of women, they asked why am I doing this because they said I looked so young. They worked for sympathy. I told them to shut up.

"Anytime I get through—I reach climax—I leave. A couple of women I cursed out while I was having sex with them. I leave, and an hour later—I might not even get home—I'd get to feelin' bad about it. Like I said, I knew I was doin' wrong, and I didn't like the idea I was actually doin' it, but I felt like I just gotta. There's one thing I ain't figured out yet is why, since I have this anger through the home life, why I gotta take it out on women. That I don't even know."

"How were you caught?"

"I was waitin' for the bus when this task force car came from behind me. The bus was about a block away. He pulled up at the curb waitin' for the light. I was lookin' at the police, and I could see their clipboards. The drawings they had, I saw that's me. So I acted like I saw somebody and walked away. But they both jumped out with their guns and told me not to move."

He grins. "At the police station they said, 'This is the boy we've been lookin' for.' They had my age from thirteen to twenty-five. I found out later they didn't actually believe there was a guy my age doin' all this. It was heavy. There was a lotta hell raised about me. There was an incident when a uniformed policeman walked in and told me, 'You're the little bastard we've been lookin' for, aren't you?' He said, 'If I had caught you I would've blown your brains out.'

"I had nine indictments. Six were for rape, and the others for attempted murder and armed robbery. The state wanted to send me up to do a lot of time, but the judge wouldn't go for it. He said I was too young."

"What made you do it again after you got out?"

He shrugs. "I didn't plan on raping. I think it was built-up frustration that finally made me do it. Things weren't actually going my way. It looked like things was tumblin' down. The job was no good, I broke up with a woman. When we broke up I thought about it three or four days. I acted like love's fool.

"It was one of those nights I started walkin'. I didn't plan the rape. I saw this woman, and I can't even describe to this day how I felt. I remember when I grabbed her she screamed lightly. I told her to shut up, and she said, 'All right, just don't hurt me.' I took her behind this building and made her take off her pants. I raped her, and then I made her give me a blow job. So then somebody came down the stairs on the other side. I made her cross the street, and she still didn't have her pants on. We went across the street behind this other building, and I committed sodomy on her and raped her again. Then I left.

"Someone must of saw us when we crossed the street. I started runnin' to a train station, and I was waitin' for the train. I threw away the jacket I had on, and I threw away the knife. But two cops came over and said they wanted to talk to me. I knew I had fucked up. I didn't want to go back to the penitentiary, so I tried to bluff my way out. It didn't work, and they arrested me.

"I was twenty then. I was just turning fifteen when I got busted the first time. In all these years I've only spent fifteen months on the street. You know," he adds reflectively, "I really didn't care about the ones I raped the first time. The woman I raped after I got out I feel bad about." He inhales deeply on a fresh cigarette.

"How so?"

"Because she came to court quite often. You know, there was always continuances. I felt bad about this. This woman probably had a good job, and she was blowin' money because of me. She had retained her own lawyer, I found out. I know she felt bad because they're saying in front of all these people at the trial that this was the woman that was raped. I felt bad that I had done it."

"Do you think women want to be raped?"

He shakes his head. "I generally don't think women want to be raped. I believe some women have their little dreams about it, but they don't actually want it to happen. Especially the women who are not around where it happens all the time, and they hear about it, and they say it's exciting. I've even known a couple of women like that. But I don't think as a whole—no."

"What advice would you give women who are confronted by a rapist?"

"I'm glad you asked that, because I've thought of this. The police is tellin' women how to take judo—they tellin' them what not to do and all this stuff. It would be better if a rapist was to tell them what was really happening. The only thing I can tell a woman is if you're confronted, don't try and fight it. Unless you're extremely good at karate, I wouldn't try fightin'. They might not be like me. This guy I know here, he wanted them to fight so he could hurt 'em. He told me, 'I got a hell of a kick when they fought. I kicked the shit out of this bitch.'

"The best thing women can do is feel along, you know? It might work if they feel along," he continues, warming to his subject. "They might be able to sane the guy. They might be able to bluff him, like sayin', 'My husband lives right here' when she might live ten miles from here. Unless she is really sure she can overpower him physically, it would be best to submit. Because a guy is out to rape, not to do physical harm. The majority of guys I talked to, they wouldn't. I know I wouldn't. If you panic him, it's just like the burglar. If you scare the burglar he might turn around and shoot you. Other than that, just feel along with it. You might run into something else worse than what's already happening.

"I wouldn't advise a woman to scream. With me it worked. She screamed, and I thought somebody might have heard, and I ran. But it's the same thing. You scream, you might scare him, and you could get hurt. If he's not up on you, scream and run. But if he's up on you, don't fight it. Submit. It's humiliating, but it's not as bad as the way everybody is thinking. If you're not pregnant, stop and think. It's not all that bad. It'll be in your mind, as it'll be in his mind. And he's sick. All you do is let yourself get sick— 'I'm a nervous wreck, and I can't mess with men anymore.' That's not cool either. But I don't think it's all that bad.

"From everything I read, rape is on the rise. Everybody's writing about it, which makes it bad for guys in here that's been here for ten years. It messes up their chances for gettin' out. It messes up their rehabilitation. They're exploiting it. They make everybody think all rapists are sex fiends, just like a dope fiend—when they want it they're gonna go get it. Do you understand? I don't believe a rapist would really repeat himself unless he got a hell of a problem that wasn't really solved and he's scared bad enough. Unless he's a guy that just gets his kicks rapin' broads, he won't repeat it. I don't believe that. It's not like a guy steady comin' back for robbery or something like that. I just don't think they repeat themselves."

"What about you? If you get out of here, are you going to repeat yourself?"

"Right now I believe I won't do it anymore. But it might be a combination of tensions and troubles and disappointments—just like a combination to a safe. If they all come together and click at the same time, it just might make me do it again. . . ."

Tom, age 30, was charged with battery and attempted rape and sentenced to four to ten years at Stateville Correctional Center in Joliet, Illinois. He served three years and two months and is currently out on parole. I interviewed him in his home.

"This might sound funny to you, but before I committed the crime I thought if a guy committed rape they should hang him by the balls and torture him to death. Then I turn around and do it. . . ."

The neighborhood verges on the seedy side—shabby rows of two-flats and run-down stores. It's a cold Saturday morning, and the overcast sky threatens snow.

Tom, wearing a colorful cowboy shirt, answers the doorbell and invites me in. He's a small, spare man with a tough ex-con's face. His dark hair is long and slicked back. After introducing me to his pregnant wife and a friend, he offers me a drink.

The apartment is large and tastefully furnished. Tom says he's doing well for himself and his family working as a mechanic. We

185

continue to make small talk, but I sense that he is tense. I know he only consented to be interviewed as a favor to a mutual friend.

"I'm ready," Tom declares abruptly. "Let's go into the other room and talk."

The room is off a long foyer and serves as Tom's den. There's a card table, a bar, and shelves adorned with beer cans from around the world. He turns on the radio to insure even more privacy.

"Doesn't your wife know about you?" I ask.

"Sure she does, but I'd rather we talk alone. What do you want to know?" He sounds a bit anxious.

"Why don't you tell me something about yourself?"

He says that he grew up in Chicago, did a stint in the army, and was married once before, for three years.

"How old are you?"

"I'm thirty. I'll be thirty-one in August."

"What led you to rape?"

"I found out in group therapy about that question. When I committed the crimes and people asked me why I did it, I couldn't answer them. I truthfully didn't know why I did it. I wasn't drunk at the time, and I wasn't on any kind of pills or dope or anything. I didn't know why. . . . I didn't.

"After I went to Stateville I got involved in group therapy. Through that I found out the reason I was doing it was proving to the men in my family that I was more of a man than they were, and proving to the women that I wouldn't be henpecked like the men were. You see, my whole family—my father would go out, and he'd work eight hours, nine hours a day, and he'd come home and clean the house, he'd do the dishes, he'd do the wash, he'd do the ironing. He had to, because if he didn't do it, it wouldn't get done." He pauses to open a beer.

"My uncle, I used to see him bust his ass in the shop and go home and sit down to a nice hot meal. He'd get halfway through with it and have to get up to take his mother-in-law someplace because she had to go someplace. And she would never ask. She says, 'Well, I'm going here or I'm going there.' And he would get up from the table, take her, and then come back to finish his supper. The supper is cold by that time.

"It was my younger childhood that actually made me do what I did in getting back at them. I remember my older sister—she's a year older than I am—when she hit sixteen she had a driver's permit. Before three months had gone by she had a license. When I hit sixteen I had to argue, beg, plead, fight, anything I could do to get my license. Two days before I went into the service I finally got my license. I was over in Germany for two years. I didn't see my family for two years. I wrote home, and I tell them I want to come home for Christmas and need a little help with the money. They can't afford to send any money at that time. I got home, and my little sister got every damn thing she wanted. Yet my mother kept telling everybody she wanted a son just like her husband." He crushes the beer can angrily.

"That's what made you rape? You wanted to get back at all the women in your life?"

He nods. "Through therapy I found out what my problem was. I found out how to handle it or cope with it—whatever you want to say. I realize that nowadays women are closer to their mother. I don't know. I don't blame women in general for what I did. Some women are domineering, but I think it's more or less the man who should put his foot down. The man is supposed to be the man. If he acts the man, the woman won't be domineering." He pops the tab on another beer.

"What were your thoughts before and after the rapes you committed?" I ask over the noise of the radio, which is blaring a country-and-western tune about lost love.

"Like I said, this is a hard question," Tom replies after a long pause. "At the time I couldn't answer it. And even now I think back about what did I think. I don't know what happened with the crime. Leave me go over the crime the way it built down, and maybe you can get an understanding of what happened.

"I was coming home from work, and I seen the woman. I don't know what attracted me to her or what. . . . I don't know what it was. But I looked at my watch, and I noticed the time. And I went home. The next day I was going home the same way, and I got to watching for the woman going into the apartment. And I looked at the time, and I noticed it was earlier than yesterday. So I parked, and I got out of the car, and I went to see if she would be by. As she came by I went into the hallway. I pulled a knife, and I put it at her throat.

"She struggled a minute or two, and she hit the door buzzer twice. Luckily nobody came down, and she seen that she couldn't get away. She said she didn't have no money. I started to feel around her, and she said, 'I'll give you what you want if you put the knife away.' So I put the knife away. She took off her panties.

187

She didn't want to lay down. I told her to stoop down, and she stooped down, and I more or less kicked her feet gently from underneath her. And she was down, and I got on top of her. I got her, got up, and left." He nervously lights a cigarette.

"Like I say, what attracted me to her I don't know. Afterwards, the reason I got busted, the reason they busted me—I went back. I thought it was an easy score. She went down easy, no fighting, no resistance—not that much fighting, not that much resistance. She gave in to me right away. I thought it was easy. I thought she liked it. So I went back to see if I could get it again, and the cops got me."

"If she had screamed or struggled more, would that have prevented you from raping her?"

"The second one I raped, I also got her in the hall with the knife up against her throat, and she froze. And I started to feel her up. She broke away and started screaming, and I ran out. The first one, if she would have been able to break away and start screaming, I probably would have run out. That would have deterred me. But like I say, she went down easy."

"Would you have used the knife?"

He shakes his head no. "Like I say, when I raped this one woman, she struggled with me for about a minute or two, something like that. But I kept my arm or my hand around her mouth, and I kept the knife up at her throat. She had my arm, holding my arm, trying to struggle, trying to move my arm away. But I kept it by her throat. But I don't think I could have used the knife. I don't think I could have hit her even. If I would have slapped her, I would have scared her more. And what I found out through different guys when I was in the penitentiary—a person can do anything, any crime to people, and get away with it if he puts enough fear into the person. If a person is scared enough, he'd do anything you tell him—man or woman." He runs his hands through his hair and shifts uncomfortably in his chair.

"Was your approach always the same?"

He nods. "I would get them in the hallway, pull out a knife, and use a knife. But that's the only way. I would never have the guts to drag someone into the alley or drag somebody into the car. It's funny, because I feel if you drag somebody in the alley, it's too easy for somebody to walk by. If you drag somebody in your car, it's too easy," he says, grinning.

"What's so funny?"

188

"I don't know if you know Chicago or not, but rapes happen right in the middle of the busiest intersections. One happened about quarter to five in the afternoon, right at rush hour. You talk about somebody coming in . . . you know?"

"Did you experience any remorse after the rapes?"

"For myself I actually didn't feel any remorse about it or anything. I felt remorse to the point where it ruined my marriage with my first wife. After I had done it and I was busted for it, then I realized how bad I hurt my wife. After I found out why I did it, I still felt real bad about it because by getting back at my family I hurt my wife worse—something I didn't want to do. I didn't want to hurt her in any way. That was the only remorse I had about the crimes themselves."

"You mean you felt nothing for your victims?"

"I didn't feel anything. I looked back when I seen the woman when I was going to court. She wasn't hurt. I know I didn't beat her. I know I didn't cut her. I know she made love before, because she had a child—I found out afterwards. There was nothing mentally. I know she wasn't hurt, so I didn't actually feel any remorse in that way."

"Did you feel she deserved it, that women ask for it?"

He shrugs. "Some women. I think some women ask for it. On the other hand, I don't think some women do."

"You said if a woman you were raping screamed, that would turn you off, right?"

He nods.

"What if a woman struggled? Would that keep you from raping her?"

"I don't think that would deter me, because like I said, when I raped the one I did rape, she did struggle with me for about a minute, minute and a half, two minutes. She was twisting around and all, trying to break free of me. I hung on to her. Like I say, I didn't cut her or hit her or anything. I just held onto her. And when she found out that she couldn't break free from me, then she gave in. But as far as struggling goes, if I had to hit her, beat her, or something like that, I think that would deter me. Like if she struggled with me and she finally stops struggling with me and I start feeling her up and she starts saying, 'No, no,' and starts to get ready to scream, and I put my hand up to stop her from screaming and she starts struggling and it seems like she's going to struggle ten to fifteen minutes without giving up—she's determined not to give in—I think that would deter me. I think that would have."

"How was it when you got out? Did people know you were a rapist?"

"My mother-in-law from the first marriage, she knows about it. She understands it, and we talk about the penitentiary and stuff like that when we get together. My wife's mother knows, but not her father. He don't know. I'm not afraid to tell him or anything, but I just feel that he don't know and there's no reason why he should know. We're already married anyway, so there's nothing he can do about it. He likes me a lot. I doubt if it would change his opinion.

"That's something that really bugged me was my feelings I would get from other people, how they would treat me. And I was really worried about when I got out. And the guy I worked with, our friendship never changed. He knew me before I went in, he knew what I went in for, everything. Our friendship was the same. In fact, I was invited to his daughter's wedding.

"My buddy, who is a scoutmaster, told me that he told all the committeemen about me before I came into the committee, so I knew he knew about it. And one night we were out drinking, and his wife turns to me and looks at me and says, 'I know where you were and why.' And I almost fell off the stool. And she looks at me and says, 'We knew about it when we met you, before we met you, and we just went by that. We seen how you act, the way you are, and we like you. What you did, that's in the past. You're not going to do it again—we can see that.' Now I'm more or less one of the family."

Tom lapses into a thoughtful silence. Outside it is beginning to snow, and on the radio someone has just won a thousand dollars.

"Will you rape again?"

He looks me directly in the eyes as he answers. "I had a chance since I've been out. I was going over to a store in the neighborhood, and I had my car parked half a block away from it. And coming back, there was a young woman—the way I like them dressed and everything, you know? And she went into the hallway, and I helped her open the door. And it flashed back in my mind what happened. And I just looked at her, and she said thank you, and I said you're welcome and turned around and walked away. The urge wasn't there. Nothing was there. I seen how she dressed, and it didn't dawn on me at the time.

"Later on that night, when I came home and I was all by

myself, it entered my mind again. And I thought, hey, that was a beautiful setup. And I didn't even think about doing it. Another thing. . . . I used to carry a knife ever since I was nine years old. Since I've been out of the joint I haven't even considered carrying a knife. I don't need them. I don't need the crutch."

"Do you think rapists should be imprisoned?"

"I think if they don't eliminate the penitentiaries, they should bring in group therapy and have more of them than what they did have when I was there. I wanted to get the help, and I went after it. In group therapy it was brought out that I was trying to get either attention or was trying to hit back at the family by doing that."

"Well, it's getting late. I know it's been hard for you to talk to me. I appreciate it."

"It's hard. I don't refuse to talk about it, because it happened. No matter what I do, I can't forget it. I have to live with it. And if I can't talk about it, I can't live with it. I know what a hellhole prison is. I know what it's like to wake up in the morning and know that I'm going to be back in that cell at night. I don't know if I'll be in one piece, if I'm going to be attacked by guys for being a rapist, or what. I don't want to go through that again. . . ."

APPENDIX

Letters from Convicted Rapists

In the course of our research we received numerous letters from the inmates we contacted, and also from inmates who heard about our project through the prison grapevine and wrote to us on their own initiative. This appendix provides a sampling of those letters. It includes a letter from Julio and three prose pieces from Sal (respectively the "Latin lover" and the sadistic rapist-murderer we interviewed at Green Haven), and five letters from inmates who declined to be interviewed but wanted to tell their stories.

Where the letters were not sent anonymously, the names of the inmates have been changed, and names or factual references in the letters have been changed or deleted. Otherwise the letters are reproduced here just as we received them. All ellipsis points appear in the originals and do not indicate omissions.

APPENDIX

"Good Evening My dear Les"

How are you? Here's sincerely hoping that when this letter reaches you it will find you in the very best thoughts of a Lady!

"Compliments of a Gentleman"

Please excuse me for refering to you by your first name however, I feel very comfortable addressing you informally. Besides, the sweetness in Life lies in dispensing with formalities.

"Thank You"

I would be more than oblige to concede a face-to face interview with you. And you would think after all these years of bottled-up idiosyncrasies your interest has uncorked!

Upon receiving your brief letter I was very shocked to know that you knew my name or that I was even convicted of "Rape" twice. I have never submitted my name to anyone in particular. Yesterday I was informed by an associate that he submitted my name in hopes the interview will be very beneficial.

My crimes are forcible rapes, sodomy and kidnapping all in the first degree . . .

Please give my letter a very warm welcome!

"Again Thank You"

Please have a very pleasant journey and enjoyed spending the evening with you having dinner by candle-lights, embraced by vivid thoughts of acquaintance!

"Good-night Les"
"Compliments of a Gentlemen"
Mr. Julio B.

195

Three pieces by Sal:

ALPHABETICAL SEX

A is for animal magnetism B is for bosom friends C is for cuckold D is for dyke E is for erogenous zone F is for frigidity G is for gentlemen prefer blondes H is for hidden persuader I is for intermission J is for joker K is for kama sutra L is for love me love my sex M is for mistress N is for nymphet O is for orgy P is for pièce de résistance Q is for quickie R is for rhythm method S is for soft center T is for transvestite U is for unexpurgated V is for voyeur W is for wife swap X is for xtramarital relationship Y is for yumping yiminy!
Z is for Zorro

UNTITLED

Let's not be in too much of a hurry, she teases, as her bed-mounting antics have you ready to climb the walls.

At last, she seems to be ready for you to sample the bridal sweet.

First she fans, then she cools your sex and your ardor.

Surely any gentleman would give a lady a chance to remove her stockings before retiring.

Your sex and your wildest fancies have been consummated, and now there she lies with that enigmatic smile.

But what did she mean by calling you the best me?

UNTITLED

He claims his dreams aren't bothering him anymore, but he can't even look at a picture without its going "funny."

And it's going on all the time. "When my grandmother came to visit, I took a Polaroid of her for me and you a album. Sixty seconds later—" Craig could not continue.

We have published ??'s postcards in a gesture of public-spirited concern.

Let the evidence serve as a reminder of the dangers of looking at too many ladies without clothes and as a warning to those who would make of me and you and sex-*hood . . . a* sex *object!*

Dear Mr. Sussman,
I'm not *interested in what you're doing, but I am interested in how you got my name and number.*
Mr. Sussman, I'm not a rapist (per se) as you think, what happen six (6) years ago I would like to forget it. But I would like to add something to your research. Both person that was involved in my case's brought the rape on themselves. . . .
I was robbing this one person apartment, she came in on me, I told her not to be afriad, to sit down, she did sit down, and the next thing I knew she was running out of the apartment screaming for help. I ran out after her, and caught her took her back to the apartment. If she wouldn't have ran, that wouldn't have happen.
And in the other case, I would say I was more the victim in this case, this person came to the door, dressed with a towel wrapped around them. I told the person to go and get some clothes on, she went into her bedroom to put some clothes on, but she put the clothes on so I could see her. I was in the other room watching her more or less so she couldn't do nothing funny, and when she started putting on clothes, there she was right in front of my eyes.
In both case's the person's brought it on there selves, running and screaming, and not fully dressed when answering the door.
Like I said, I'm not interested in what you're doing. I guess today was the first time I really thought about them case's, and why did I do it. So now I guess I can stop searching within for now I know who was wrong.
Mr. Sussman, I hope this short note helps you as it helped me to realize something about myself.
Thank you,

·   *I am*

Felix P.

On Nov 23, 19,75 I was picked up for rape of a 4. year old Baby when I was into the Back of the room making a long distance call to Calif to let my friends no that I have made it home alright when this youge man was into the hall way where I did not see him, so he went into the bedroom with this little Gril & raped her, so she was cryin but I did not no what was happening in there, so I keep on callin to Calif, but at that time the little Gril mother came home from work at the door when he came out to let her in the house when she saw her little Gril just layin there she asked who did this to her little Gril & he toled her it was me & I said it was him, so the police man came to my home and picked me up for rape, Now if I would have raped someone I no better to go to my house No Way because I no that will be the first place they will come you no, dig this I had about ten ladies out there that loved me so rapin was not put out for me to do you no, and the raper are still out there havein his fun when I am just hopin to see 88–98 so I can get out there with the lil life that will be left into me you no, so I hope to be herein from you again okay

Your Sincerely
Roland W.

RAPE

"You have got to be kidding," stated my father the first time he came to see me in jail, "did't I teach you better than to do something like that." Sure dad sure you not only taught me not to, but you helped me to live in a society that not only adheres to such a thing, but is also based on concepts that derive from societies that have these ideals. I know all inmates blame there cases on society. I do not clame to be an exception. This is one problem that has been around along time. The only solution I see is in the minds of men. We must teach our children to not even think of such a thing. We must wipe it off the face of the earth.

Where do people problems start? Well, mine started at home; after my parents split up I felt that I was all alone because with out both a mother and father I could not grow up to be a full man. Why was I put here in the first place, I know that it was not to do the things that I have done. . . .

Now let us go to the root of the problems that this society has. We live in a society that adheres to weak and loose morals. A society that is luxury loving and highly materialistic; thrill seekers; self worshipers; highly rich, criminal, oppressive and racist. These ideals come from a Social Order that was rooted in Roman pagamism and mythology. After a study of this society one gets the picture that man has not progressed.

Why can't I base my actions on this society? I feel that my problem started at college. They told me to forget all that I learned in high school; that was alright, but it seems that I left my morals in high school also. Sex does not excite me enough to want to take someone against her will. Being an ex-G.I. I can say that I left the rest of my morals in there. The type of woman that one sees close to an Army base is the type that I don't even want to be close to me. These women are low and dirty and likes to be treated that way. I could not see myself treating anyone like that, so I left.

I am the type of person who likes to be there when someone needs help; I like to please my woman. Even the woman I raped I was trying to please, and I am quite sure that I did. I feel that the last ounce of respect for society left me when I left jail for the first time. I was very bitter because of the way I was treated, and because I felt that I was still in a prison after I left.

That brings us to my case. I feel sorry, not for myself but for the woman that I raped. I know that she has thought about the way she was treated for those few minutes. She will have mental scares that will never leave her. After trying to get something for nothing for so long one starts to get everything for nothing. While in the process I thought this was easy, I didn't even have to talk for hours or even days, or weeks even. On my case it was not by force it was more by suggestion, of course without full concent it is by force.

Being locked up for a rape charge is another thing altogether. Once the other inmates find out what your charge is they start to ask questions and the silly ones start to tease you and call you tree-jumper. This was the first time I was called an artist in my life. Alot of people wanted to fight because they have wives, dauthers, and mothers that they have to think about. I feel that someone who rapes another should be given enough time to think about his actions. I think like this because I have three sisters and alot of cousins that I really care for.

APPENDIX

Dear Mr. Sussman and Ms. Bordwell,

I hope you can use this letter about my life. I am serving time here and I hope you'll be interested in my story.

I was raised in a south side section of Chicago, the oldest of five children. My mother is a kind women, my father an alcholic, he used to beat us kids with a broom or his belt when ever we did the slightest little thing to irrate him, and that wasn't very much either. He is just plain mean, or I should say that he was, he has mellowed sum in his 60 years on this earth. My mother is 50 years old, a 10 year difference.

I am 30, my sister 29, my brother 28, my other sister 27, and my baby brother is 25.

I wasn't really a bad kid when I was a teen. I was sixteen the first time that I was arrested, for burglary of an empty building. I was released to my parents the same day because the owner asked the police to let me go since this was my first time in trouble. That was in February of 1963, but soon my life in crime was to begin. You see, my father didn't treat me as he did the rest of my brothers and sisters, because when he married my mother she was pregnant already by another man. My father knew this, but he still married her anyway. I guess that after they were married awhile he started to hate me for being a bastard child, and not really being of his own making. He used to take my brother and sister out in this big vacant lot and teach them how to operate his car, but he wouldn't let me behind the wheel. This got me mad, and so having run away from home a few times, I decided to run away again, only this time I would take his car, boy would that get him mad, and I thought at the same time that this was one way into which to get even with him for all the beatings he had given me.

So having just gotten out of trouble in February I had gotten into trouble in May of the same year (1963), I stole

202

APPENDIX

*his car with two of my friends and we hit route 66 with
California on our minds. However we had only seven
dollars between us, and that didn't take us very far, we
need gas and money, so we stopped in this town of Streator
Ill, because one of the times that I had run away, I met a
guy who lived their and remembered where his house was
located. When we got their he wasn't home so we pulled
into a gas station and I tryed to sell my dad's handdrill
and saw to the operator for some gas. He told us to wait
til the owner came, we waited but the police came instead.
We were brought back to Chicago by the Chicago police
dept, and two of us were lodged in the Audy home because
we were only 16 years old, and the other guy was taken
to the county jail, he was 17.*

    *I didn't know anything about dope, sex, (male or
female relationships) I didn't smoke, drink or cuss even,
I was scared, the guards used to hit us in the head with a
wet towel for talking to one another, it was a bad expe-
riance for me and I wanted out bad. I promised God that
I would be good if he helped me get out of this jam, and
I cryed alot too. When I had gone to court a number of
times I was sure that I would be released, but on my last
and final court date, my father told the judge "Lock him
up a while longer, maybe ita do him some good." It sure
did. I blame, or used to blame this first incarceration period
for me getting into all of my other troubles with the law,
but now I know that its just me, thats what I think anyway.
I was locked up from May of 1963 til March of 1964 and
released on perole from St Charles reform school. I was
17 years old now, I was a man, I had learned to fight and
take no bull shit from anyone, and I wouldn't ever listen
to my parents again, I'm my own boss now.*

    *When I got home I was soon to be engaging in fist
fights with my dad and mom, and my brothers and sisters
too. I hooked up with a few guys whom I had met in the
reform school and soon I was trained on how to steal cars
by popping the lock with a screw driver. I was out only
2½ months when I got busted and sentenced to 10 days in
the house of corrections. I was released on Wednesday,
and arrested the very next day for a concealed weapons
charge, I had a 20 inch bayonet on my person, I made*

*bond which was only 50 dollars and when it was time to
go to court, I failed to show up. I was arrested July 7th
and put into that jungle they call cook county jail, I spent
another 7½ months in the youth commission, I was trans-
fered their from the cook county jail because I was only
17 and on perole from their, I was released in January
of 1965 from St Charles and stayed out only 44 days, I
was arrested this time for 21 counts of burglary, auto theft
and aggravated assault, I spent another 8 months locked
up in the youth commission, this time at Sheridan, I went
to St Charles at first, stayed their only 31 days and ex-
caped, got caught four days later in Chicago, and sent to
Sheridan. In 1966 I did 6 months in the cook county jail
for auto theft, and in 1967 I was sentenced to 1-10 years
in the state penitentary for attempted burglary, I spent 34
months in Stateville, being released on perole in March of
1970. During the time I was peroled, and the time I spent
out on the streets, (five years) I have gotten married, have
a child five years old, turned into an alcholic and sometimes pill popper, worked at least 25 jobs the longest being
17 months, the shortest 1½ days, have engaged in sex with
other women while being married (18 in all), and caught
the clap twice, from two different women. My wife never
found this out because I was on the run for seven months
with this here warrent for rape in other parts of the country.
I was caught in Texas, or to put it right, I called the police
their and turned my self in. I was tired of running. What
led me to commit this act, I don't know, I can only tell
you how it came about. This is how it happened.*

Sept 23rd 1976
   *I had been out now for three days drinking and smok-
ing reefer with two of my buddies whom I'll refer to as
A and B. A and B are brothers, we really got messed up,
and now we were sitting in A's apartment stone broke and
trying to collect our thoughts together. A and B's cousin
came over, he is a heroin addict, and tells us that he has a
dealers home address, and that the guy got 5 thousand
dollars in his house. A and B just robbed this same guy
three weeks earlier for 3,200 dollars while this dealer was
walking the streets. Well, how could we turn down this,
by the way we were all still pretty high when we did this*

job, almost drunk you might say. I just knew that I didn't have a job any more because three days had gone by and I didn't bother to call in, plus I hadn't called my wife either, plus my rent was now due, and my car payment was due soon too, so here I sit, broke, high and in need for some capital. The junkie gave us the address, then we cut some nylons to put over our heads, I had a pump sawed off 20 gauge shot gun right their at A's house so we had everything nesseary to go over their and rob this dealer's house. Their wasn't any plans to rape this women, it just happened. We drove over their, looked the house over and left, B borrowed 10 dollars from some guy he knew and bought 4 six packs of beer, and the four of us drank them down while we drove back to the house.

    By the time we got their it was dark. I don't have any idea what time it was because I was high, but I'll say between 8pm and midnite. We parked the car down the street and A-B and I proceeded towards the house, A with the shot gun, B and I with nothing but the thought of some quick money. I remember saying to myself that this is just ripping off a dope dealer and he isn't any good any way, sort of justifying the crime, so I thought.

    The junkie stayed in the car. Since A and his brother B just ripped off this guy, they wanted me to knock on the door. Well I couldn't wear my nylon mask for that, who would open the door seeing someone standing their with a mask on?, so I knocked while they hid around the corner of the building. I knocked twice before this guy pulled up the shade and peeked out at me. He said "what do you want," I said, "I want to make a deal," he said, "what kind of deal," I said that I was sent their by a friend of his and that I needed to fix bad, please could he just open the door so I wouldn't have to talk so loud, and he did, wide open, he invited me in and just as I walked in, A and B rushed in behind me. The guy ran into his living room where their were two of his buddies sitting on the couch. A gave me the shotgun as we ran in after this guy and I told him and his friends to "hit the rug with their noses." the three of them complyed, I gave B the shotgun and tore this phone off the wall, and when I did that I noticed some stairs leading up from the kitchen, and their was a purse sitting

APPENDIX

on them. I told A to go up stairs and check it out, while he did that I started hog tieing these guys and asking them where the money was.

After I had tied the last one up, A came down stairs with this women, she was about 50, and didn't have anything on but a see thru negilgie, and the pillow case that A had put over her head. He layed her down, and I sat on her buttocks and as I was tying her hands behind her back, my thing got hard. I like the feel of silk and this turned me on but I still hadn't thought about raping her, not until B pulled her panties off and started playing with her vagina. These guys couldn't or wouldn't tell us where all this money was supposed to be, and I said to myself, "Fuck it, if we get caught, I'll be put away for a long time so it doesn't matter what I do," so I took this women back upstairs to the darkened bedroom and untied her hands, and told her to ly on the bed, which she did, she was very coopertive and did everything I told her to do. Even if she had struggled I most likly would have been very appressive and raped her anyway for the following reasons,

1. I have had a very full sex life, and I have a strong sex drive.

2. Being under the influence of alcohol, I would have taken her because when I am drunk I tend to be aggressive anyway, I get mean, and like most people who over indulge, I get the desire for sexual contact.

3. I would probably have tried to knock her out, and then proceed to rape her altho I was drunk, I don't think that I would have killed her, but I can't honestly say that I wouldn't have.

Afterwards A didn't like what I had done, B wanted to have sexual intercourse with her too, A wouldn't let him and I didn't want him to either because after I brought her back down stairs and hog tied her, I stepped back and looked at her, how afraid she was, and it was then that I felt remorse and ashamed of what I'd done to her and when he walked over to her and put his hand on her ass, I suddenly felt mad, mad at myself for what I'd just done, and I didn't want her to go thru this degrading experience again. If this had happened to my mother, wife or two sis-

ters, I would feel that I'd have to kill whoever did this, even if I had to wait twenty years to do it.

Anyway, we didn't get the 5,000 dollars, we only got $250 and some grass, we were in that house for about an hour I guess, and after we had left and were driving back to A's apartment, I remember thinking to myself, my god, what have you done. It wasn't only the robbery that affected me, it was the rape too, the rape more so. I seemed to sober up all of a sudden, and started feeling guilty about it. To this day I feel bad that I subjected a person to this degrading offence. B got caught 4 day's latter, A got caught 5 months latter and I turned myself in 7 months later. How did we get caught? The junkie got arrested two days after the rape and robbery and turned us in to get off the hook on a posession of narcotics charge.

You see how the rape came about now, we had just planed to rob that dealer and leave, their wasn't any premeditation about rape, it just happened. But even tho I hate to admit that I did rape a woman, regardless of the circumstances, when you forcefully violate another persons body, you're a rapist, their are no ifs, ands, or buts about it. My sexual relationship with my wife wasn't all that hot then, she was always getting sick, and was in and out of the hospital, she couldn't take birth control pills, because when she did use them she ended up getting a blood clot on her lung, and she was fat, and I didn't enjoy that extra flab between us when we were making love. This women was thin, and I could ly flat on top of her and feel her body, her whole body, right next to mine. I just couldn't get any sexual satisfaction with my wife.

Like I said, after I had committed this act, I felt bad. I wanted to call this women and tell her that I'm sorry and that I wasn't in my right mind. I would have just said that I was drunk and didn't know what I was doing and that I'm sorry. I mean, what else could I say? You can't undo what is already done. But how could I do that? I was sorry, yeh, but I couldn't get myself to call her, I just wanted to close my mind to what I'd done, forget about it like it never happened. I sometimes believed I didn't do it either, but I know that I did, it has been two years now since this happened and I still feel bad about what I've done.

APPENDIX

They say that the motivation for rape can be a desire to be sexually dominate, or that you may have guilt feelings about sex, and that by forceful raping of a woman your guilt feeling can be erased and sexual activity enjoyed because the raped person is forced into sex, and therfore will submit to your demands. This may be true. I would say that I enjoyed the sexual contact at the time of the rape, but *afterwards when I sobered up, I did regret this act, I even hated myself for about a year, but now I'm over this period of self hate, and I'm finished with this way of life. I had always stolen with a clear, sober mind, but I know for a fact that if I hadn't been drunk, I certainly wouldn't have done that robbery and I certainly wouldn't have raped that woman. All that I can say is that I'm sorry that I did this to her, and that even tho this may be impossible for her, I hope that she doesn't think about this incident again. The crime of rape is one of the most degrading things that can happen to a person, this is my honest opinion be it male or female. I have seen grown men get gang raped while incarcerated in these various prisons, and I hate those people who do this to another human being, I hate them enough to just about kill them. Maybe this is what should happen to me, then I wouldn't have to live with this shame hanging over my head.*

This is my life, my crime, and my thoughts, and I swear that everything is true of what I have written, but Please! *don't use my name, as I don't want to bring back the suffering and shame my wife, child and family have suffered, and if you decide that you can't use this material then I would appreciate it if you just burn it, because I wouldn't want prison officials here to read this as they open all incoming mail.*

Respectfully,

Richard G.

P.S. If you do decide to use this material, you can change it somewhat, as I know that I'm no pen man.

APPENDIX

As always in a story of this descript nature the author usually remains annyonomous, as I will do here since I am so to say, not completely proud of that fact that I am a person who has committed a crime that is called by society, "henious," although I do not completley agree with this "label," I still feel that revealing my true identity would cause adverse affects on my future life, as society, or certain members of society will never let me forget that I am one of the elite in the criminal catagory, a rapist. . . .

But I can start my piece here by saying that I trully don't believe I am what you would call a rapist, maybe someone who just at the time took gross advantage of an unwilling subject in the course of sexual intercourse. The reasons why, and the hows and wherefores are still for me slightly hard to put into words, as in my case, emotions and deprvity were my motivators, and a mind not yet fully matured in matters of women and sex.

For years, in fact, even before I can remember, I was surrounded and brought up by women, namely my mother and three sisters. Soon after I was born in 1947 my so-called father decided that he to was surrounded by women, to the point where he just had to leave it all behind, at least this is what my mother led me to believe, and one sister one thing, and the other another concept, and even my dear younger sister had her own version. But I found out much later, and after much confusion, that I myself even came up with MY own reason why I grew up fatherless.

At the time of my adolescence I thought that it was pretty nice to have either my mother or one of my sisters go out of their way to do something for me, like who would cook my breakfast or come into the bathroom to make sure I washed up good and brushed my teeth and all that, and even better I thought to go and make sure that they too had done what they were supposed to do. When I got a little older and a little wiser and informed to women and what they were really about, it got even better for me, or

209

should say worse, but I thought it was pretty nice to be able to see my sisters and mother around the house, especially in the summer, when they would say how hot it was while walking around the house in the underwear, and alot of times, without even that. At those times my mind would fanticize to the point of things that I thought were only in Playboys and things, like taking my sister or even my mother. And I can't really say why rape or incest didn't occur at those times, because I used to dream of having my sisters more than once, more than a hundred times in fact.

I could hardly wait for summer time to come, this is now when I'm just in High School and in my teens, so I could go check out the windows and gangways, peeping toming they call it, and I used to just love that, to peep through the little cracks in the drapes and watch women undress, or when I was lucky, to see them with whoever the men were, having sexual intercourse. As I think back to those times now, I still don't feel that there was nothing really wrong with that, I mean, I wasn't really doing anything, and it surly made me feel good. Sometimes I used to walk miles, and look into hundreds of windows looking for the right scenes. It seemed that after the first time I peeped at a woman undressing, or making love, it obsessed me to see more of the same thing, but mostly all the time, to see more, and longer. It would excite me and cause me to be relieved, but just for a little while, until I got home and was around the family, and laying in my bed wondering if my sister would say anything if I went in her room and got in bed with her, or make up some stories to go to my mother with so I could get close to her and maybe make her feel sorry for me or something so she'd carress me or ask me to lay down with her. But for some reason that I can't to this day figure out, there was never any physical contact between myself or my sisters or mother. I just can't explain why not because most of my desires and feelings for these women used to keep me up at nights, and upset me quite a bit at times.

After I quit highschool I had my share of women and relationships and whatever, but still had my obsession to see a beautiful woman in my own way, and do things in my own way. Because although I was somewhat older now, in my early twenties, I still had to have my secret meetings at the windows in the night, and it just got better as I got older. Maybe I shouldn't say better, but the excitement was intencified, and my satisfaction was growing to a point where I needed more. I guess you can say that it got to be a habit, and satisfying myself was getting harder and harder to do just looking through windows. I had to participate . . . I had to be the one she was with. She was anyone then. I wasn't so particular anymore. I saw big ones, small ones and not so beautiful anymore, but the pretty ones were my favorites.

The first girl that I felt you could say I raped was what you could say a friend of a friend, and at this time my indroctination into some thing altogether different than just looking through windows and dreaming. In this sense I actually mean putting some of my fantisys into reality, and experiencing the feeling of complete dominence, of which dominence I believe is the most important factor and main contributor in the mind of a rapist, at least thats how I felt. . . . But I was introduced to this girl, named Joyce at a party at a friends house one summer night, and as usual, at parties where at that time it was considered "hep" to partake of more than just fruit punch, we all were having a good time, and being with this girl, dancing, being close to her most of the night excited me to the point to where I was playing out the whole role, of what I'd like to do to this girl, and nothing more, just what I'd do to her, and how I'd do it. So one thing led to another and it was decided that we'd all go to my friends house to sit around and have a few more drinks and listen to some music, but of course my friend and I had different ideas, and I'm sure both the girls kind of knew themselves that we'd do more than just that. As it was, Joyce and I hit it off pretty good, and were'nt in the house more than a few minutes before we were rolling around on the couch necking like crazy. That was all I needed, I was so worked up that even tho we still had all our clothes on I managed to climax, but it seemed that Joyce wasn't as free and easy as she played to be because when I made suggesstive moves to really get it on, she changed into the protective

211

holier than thou type that changed my excitement into almost rage. By this time my friend and his girl were already in the bedroom and having a nice time, which made me even more hostile towards this tramp that was teasing me.

I felt confused, and that I had to do something to even the score so to say, and what was worse, she could see that I was angry but still stuck to her role. At first she didn't try to stop me when I tore her blouse off, I guess she didn't think I was serious or something, and she didn't protest or scream or any thing until I forced her down and tried to push her skirt up, she knew then that I was'nt playing and tried to get up and go, by this time I was worked up to a passion that I don't think anything could've stopped except the actual act, and her protests egged me on all the more. Now I wasn't trying anymore, but pulling and ripping and holding her by the throat down. I think she realized that there wasn't any use in her strugglling anymore, that is until I ripped her panties off and was taking my pants off with one hand, then she knew that wasn't the way she wanted it. Now I don't think anything else was in my mind but taking this girl, anyway I could. I proceeded to have sexual intercourse with her, but felt cheated because she still persisted to struggle, but it seemed that more pressure I put to her throat, the more docile she became. Force her, and theres nothing she could do. I wasn't satisfied with myself and wanted more. I believe that if she would have just submitted and not struggled, I might've gave up on the whole idea. But as it was as soon as I'd let my hand go from her throat, she'd feel that was it and try to get up and go, I just didn't feel she was payed back, besides satisfying myself was the only thing on my mind. She fought when I turned her over and stuck my finger up her backside, and even more when I actually violated her. But that was it, I just didn't feel there was any more use, and I got up. She slowly got off the couch and got dressed and said that she didn't think I was that kind and that was it. I saw her alot of times after that, but never said anything to her nor her to me. And nothing more was ever said about it.

I didn't feel as tho I accomplished anything, and was

very excited at first with the thought in my mind that I'm in command. I guess that she just wasn't a good subject.

This was quite some time ago, and as I've stated, somewhat of a new experience that I thought nothing of, and trully felt that that was the way it was supposed to be. I enjoyed seeing her want her freedom, and not being able to do anything about the fact that I was taking her against her will.

But that was nothing compared to the excitement I experienced in my dominent role, which came about you could say by accident, nothing was planned or pre arranged or anything like that. I was simply driving one night about 9:30 in the evening and picked up a sweet young thing who was hitchiking down one of the North side streets. She wasn't going far, but almost as soon as she got in the car I pulled over, I kind of jokingly told her that the ride was going to cost her, she knew exactly what I meant and said a couple choice words and went for the door, I grabed her around the upper arm and put one hell of a hold on her that made her turn colors. All I did then was unzip my fly and she took the hint. I felt superior, I felt like woman were nothing more than an object to use sexually, in whatever way, and however, and when ever. This time my excitement was at a peak because this young girl, who wasn't more than 17, was actually trembling with fright. This added to my excitement, and I quickly climaxed. With no after thought of doing a thing wrong, in fact I felt that, to me, I was doing her a service. Please don't misunderstand me, I was fully aware that the law was being broken, but I didn't care, and never expected to get caught or found out. These types of experiences happened 6 more times within a one year period, with most all of them ending up the same way, after my threat, they were in my command. I used to threaten murder, slicing their throats with a knife I produced, which was the best, it excited me to see the fright and sheer dominence I had over each and every one of them.

But it seemed that with each new experience, I was missing something, and that it could get even better, and that I could experience even more satisfication.

What cause me to my final end here in the penten-

tiary was this sickness that eroded my mind over the years, and the complete disregard for the law I aquired by never once having any doings with the law for ever violating any of the some 15 women I assalted or raped.

I didn't want to have to wait to pick up women off the streets hitchiking or from taverns, but I got to the point that when I had the desire for a woman, I had to have her then, and I knew my method of threats and violence always seemed to work, all the time.

At times I knew that I was going to be caught, but then again I didn't. Its kind of hard to explain, but when the desire motivated me, I had no cares or worries about the police. I got bold and out of my head at times, I was at the point now of actually following women when they would get off the bus to see where they lived, not just one, but up to as many as 9. Where I would drive to a place near their homes and wait until one would come out preferrably during the night time. After I waited an hour or so, I'd go to one of the others and wait there until she'd come out to go to the store or whatever. And now I was choosey, I picked up some real beauties who I thought would be the utmost in satisfaction. I was more and more driven, because in one night I had three women until I felt satisfied. All in the manner mentioned above.

This seemed so easy a way, to spot the girl, and drive up and wait by the alley way faking car trouble, and when she was near, just pull her off the street into the car and drive off down streets where I wouldn't have to stop for lights or anything, and usually telling the girl I wouldn't hurt her to keep her calm. I'd usually wind up at the forest preserves where I could make a night of it with the girl in every way. I became more degenerate, the normal proceedure for intercourse was usually my last step in the act, firstly making her do all the things she dispised most. I was at the peak of obtaining the satisfaction I desired. I was even a gentleman about the whole thing, when I was done, and even after having conversations with alot of those girls, I'd drive them almost to their doorstep.

Even for these girls, most of them any way, never did they protest after the act was done, but would just sit there in the car while I'd be driving them and talk about, and how depraved I was, and I should've just asked and things like that. Which made me even more ignorant of the fact that these girls were telling the law.

Three women pressed charges against me for rape after police arrested me through photographs these ladys had provided them with.

At the time of my arrest I had the feeling that everything was over, and that would be it, but it went much deeper than that. I couldn't pinpoint any one reason for my acts, except that of confusion when I knew it was over with, and that I'd go to jail. I knew that I'd done something serious, but then again I didn't think I had.

As a result of my arrest, I was convicted and sentenced to 15 to 45 years in prison for rape, aggravated kidnapping, aggravated assault, and deviate sexual assault.

I would also like to add that since my incarceration in 1973, I have had one talk with a medical doctor at the time of my reception into this prison system, since that time I have been treated as any other inmate, and have recieved no kind of counseling, guidence or whatever, except through my own endeavors.

My career as a rapist is over. . . .

DATE DUE

DEC 2 9 1983			
JAN 1 2 1984			
NOV 2 9 1984			
JAN 3 1 1985			
APR 0 0 1986			
DEC 1 1 1986			
OCT 1 3 1988			
APR 0 6 1993			
APR 1 3 1999			
APR 1 9 2002			
MAY 2 0 2002			